FAST FACTS ON
FALSE TEACHINGS

Ron Carlson / Ed Decker

HARVEST HOUSE PUBLISHERS
Eugene, Oregon 97402

Cover by Left Coast Design, Portland, Oregon

FAST FACTS ON FALSE TEACHINGS

Copyright © 1994 Harvest House Publishers
Eugene, Oregon 97402

Library of Congress Cataloging-in-Publication Data

Carlson, Ron, 1950–
    Fast facts on false teachings / Ron Carlson & Ed Decker.
      p. cm.
    ISBN 1-56507-168-9
    1. Cults—Controversial literature 2. Christian sects—Controversial literature.
    3. Christianity and other religions. I. Decker, Ed. II. Title.
BP603.C36 1994
291.9—dc20
                                              93-43729
                                                  CIP

Printed in the United States of America.

00 01 02 03 / BP / 15 14 13 12 11 10

*To Dr. Walter Martin,
our long-time friend and mentor, who
encouraged and inspired us both to always
"contend for the faith" (Jude 3)*

Contents

Why Defend the Faith?

———————— ◆ ————————

The presentation of apologetics isn't always popular. A cultist isn't going to be thrilled that *you* now know things he wishes you never did, and even many of your fellow Christians will frown upon your newfound zeal to defend the faith. In fact, you might be amazed at the number of well-meaning Christians who find the defense of the faith just too embarrassing and negative for them to even try out. They say, "It's too unloving. God sees these people's hearts. Who are we to judge?" So they stand by and let a lie become the norm because they will not speak out with a defense for the doctrines and purity of our faith.

Let's start right out by defining the world of Christian apologetics and polemics.

Apologetics: Systematic argumentative discourse in defense, as of a doctrine. Defense of the faith.

Polemics: An aggressive attack on or refutation of the opinions or principles of another, as in denouncing heresy.

The Bible tells us in Jude 3:

> Dear friends, although I was very eager to write to you about the salvation we share, I felt I had to write and urge you to contend for the faith that was once for all entrusted to the saints.

Paul tells us in Philippians 1:7:

> It is right for me to feel this way about all of you, since I have you in my heart; for whether I am in chains or defending and confirming the gospel, all of you share in God's grace with me.

In 2 Timothy 2:15 Paul says:

> Do your best to present yourself to God as one approved, a workman who does not need to be ashamed and who correctly handles the word of truth.

He says further in 2 Timothy 4:2:

———————

> Preach the Word; be prepared in season and out of season; correct, rebuke and encourage—with great patience and careful instruction.

Peter also declares this same message in 1 Peter 3:15:

> In your hearts set apart Christ as Lord. Always be prepared to give an answer to everyone who asks you to give the reason for the hope that you have.

With these biblical exhortations in mind, we see that *it is our Christian duty to fulfill our commission from the Lord.* We become defenders of the faith as we witness to those lost in darkness, and especially to those who bring those false teachings to the world that we seek for Christ.

Defending the Faith in Israel

In the biblical account of Elijah's encounter with the prophets of Baal, we find that Baal worship had been introduced into Israel. So Elijah stood before the people and cried out:

> How long halt you between two opinions? If the Lord be God, follow him: but if Baal, then follow him.

He then challenged the prophets of Baal to call down fire from Baal upon the sacrifice that they had prepared. Although they called on Baal from morning to evening, leaping upon the altar and slashing themselves, nothing happened.
Elijah derided them by saying:

> Cry aloud: for he is a god; either he is talking, or he is pursuing, or he is in a journey, or peradventure he sleepeth, and must be awakened.

Then Elijah called down fire from God, which consumed not only the sacrifice but also the altar stones and the water in the ditch around the altar (1 Kings 18).

What Did Jesus Say?

In Matthew 12:34,39 Jesus said this to the religious leaders of His day:

> You brood of vipers, how can you who are evil say anything good? . . . A wicked and adulterous generation asks for a miraculous sign.

In Matthew 13:15 He continued:

> For this people's heart has become calloused; they hardly hear with their ears, and they have closed their eyes. Otherwise they might see with their eyes, hear with their ears, understand with their hearts and turn, and I would heal them.

In Matthew 15:7 He called the scribes and Pharisees "hypocrites," and in verse 9 He said:

> They worship me in vain; their teachings are but rules taught by men.

In Matthew 21 He connected the parable of wicked husbandmen with the religious leaders of Israel. In Matthew 23:23-25,27,28,33 He said:

> Woe to you, teachers of the law and Pharisees, you hypocrites! You give a tenth of your spices—mint, dill and cummin. But you have neglected the more important matters of the law—justice, mercy and faithfulness. You should have practiced the latter, without neglecting the former. You blind guides! You strain out a gnat but swallow a camel. Woe to you, teachers of the law and Pharisees, you hypocrites! You clean the outside of the cup and dish, but inside they are full of greed and self-indulgence.
> . . . Woe to you, teachers of the law and Pharisees, you hypocrites! You are like whitewashed tombs, which look beautiful on the outside but on the inside are full of dead men's bones and everything unclean. In the same way, on the outside you appear to people

as righteous but on the inside you are full of hypocrisy
and wickedness.
    You snakes! You brood of vipers! How will you
escape being condemned to hell?

All too many people are willing to hear the words of
peace and faith from Jesus but are reticent to hear the Jesus
who upbraided those teachers who would lead their followers into darkness (Matthew 15:14).

The Apostles Speak Out

The apostles and disciples of Jesus also boldly rebuked
the false teachers of their day. The first of these apologists,
Peter in Acts 2:14-41; 3:12-26; 4:8-12 and Stephen in Acts
6:8-10; 7:1-60, spoke forcefully against the unbelieving Jews.
    In Acts 13:8-12 Paul condemned sorcery. He spoke against
the Jewish leaders in Acts 13:16-46; 14:1-4; 17:1-4 and rea-
soned with them out of the Scriptures in their synagogues.
In Acts 17:16-34 Paul contended with the Jews and then
against paganism with the Greeks. Then to the Galatians
he defended his apostleship and the teaching of grace
against the Judaizers.

The Early Church Fathers

The strong words of correction did not end with Christ
and the apostles. After they were gone from the scene,
great men of God rose up to defend the church even when
to do so was considered illegal.
    First these men had to defend the faith against the Jews,
and then later against paganism and later heresies. The
first of these were Quadratus, Bishop of Athens, and Aris-
tedes, philosopher of Athens, who wrote a defense of
Christianity addressed to Emperor Hadrian about 117 A.D.
    Between 117 and 138 A.D., Hegesippus wrote about the
heresies of Simeon, Cleobus, Gorthoeus, Masbotheus, Me-
nander, Marcion, Carpocrates, Valentinus, Basilides, and
Saturnilius, and also the Jewish heresies of the Essenes,
Galileans, Hemereobaptists, Samaritans, Sadducees, and
Pharisees.

Later Justin Martyr wrote his first apology to Emperor Antonius Pius about 138 A.D. Tatian wrote against the Greeks about 163 A.D. Justin wrote his second apology to the emperors, his dialogue with Trypho (to the Jews), and his hortatory address to the Greeks. At about this time Athenagoras and Tatian wrote their apologies.

Melito of Sardis wrote a discourse to Emperor Antonius around 166 A.D. During the same period Dionysius of Corinth and Philip of Gortyna wrote against Marcion, and Theophilus of Antioch wrote against Marcion and others. Apollinaris, Bishop of Hierapolis, wrote five books against the Greeks, two books against the Jews, and another against the Phrygian heresy and Montanus. Musanus Modestus (disciple of Justin) wrote an elegant work to some of the brethren who had swerved from the truth to the heresy of the Encratites and Tatianus.

Irenaeus, Tertullian, and Origen

Between 170 and 220, Irenaeus, Bishop of Lyons, wrote "On Knowledge" against the Greeks and also "Against Heresies" or "Overthrow of False Doctrine," in which he outlined and refuted the doctrines of the Gnostics, including Simon Magus, Cerinthus, Valentinus, Marcion, and others.

In approximately 180 A.D., Rhoto, a disciple of Tatian, wrote against Marcion and other false teachers. Miltiades the historian wrote against Montanus and the Paraphrygian heresy of Montanism. Apollonius of Rome wrote against the Phrygian heresy and Montanus. Serapion, Bishop of Antioch, wrote against the Phrygians.

Around 194 Tertullian wrote his apology, and in 205 Clement of Alexandria refuted the Greek Heresiarchs. Between 205 and 250 Origen had discourse with Beryllus, winning him back from heresy to the truth. He wrote a reply against Celsus the Epicurian called "The True Doctrine," and is also credited with debating the Arabians and later the Helcisaites, leading many of these back to orthodoxy. Between 250 and 256 Cyprian of Carthage wrote against Novatus and Cornelius of Rome wrote against Novatus and the heresies of the Cathari.

Apologetics in the Councils

During this same period, Dionysius, Bishop of Alexandria, wrote against the Novatians, the Sabellians, and later the schism of Nepos. At the Council of Antioch a former Sophist refuted Paul of Samosata. In 314, the Council of Arles was held against the Donatists, and in 325, the Council of Nicea was held to deal with the Arian heresy.

These are just some of the church fathers up to Nicea who defended the faith against the Jews, paganism, and heresies. Had it not been for their polemic and apologetic works, we would know little indeed of these great men from the first four centuries of Christianity, as this sort of defense of the faith makes up the greater part of their extant writings.

God Calls the Reformers

In addition to these, a host of great men from every age (such as Augustine and Martin Luther) have spoken out against heresies, excesses, and misuse of power inside and outside the church.

Not a few of them died martyrs' deaths to defend the faith we take for granted!

Among the tenets they so vigorously defended were:

> the deity of Christ
> the trinity
> the sovereignty of God
> the inerrancy of Scripture
> the depravity of man
> salvation as a free gift through faith in Christ
> the certainty of final judgment.

They also wrote against Gnosticism, a terrible heresy which is again creeping into Christian doctrine.

Apologists in Our Time

In our own age, men like Charles Finney and Dwight L. Moody have spoken out against Freemasonry in the church and immorality, thereby taking a strong stand for the faith.

Today, apologetics has broadened to encompass many different fields in the defense of historic biblical Christianity. Some of the leading apologists for the defense of the faith include C.S. Lewis, who was a great *literary* apologist; Francis A. Schaeffer, who was a *philosophical* apologist; Walter Martin, who was a modern pioneer in *religious and cult* apologetics; Henry Morris, who specializes in *scientific* apologetics in the defense of creation; Josh McDowell, who enunciates *historical* apologetics; John Warwick Montgomery, who uses *legal* principles to defend Christian truth; and Charles Colson, who articulates *cultural* apologetics in defense of the timeless absolutes given by God.

To these and many more we owe a personal debt of gratitude. Today we stand with those who have gone before us and say:

> I am not ashamed of the gospel, because it is the power of God for the salvation of everyone who believes: first for the Jew, then for the Gentile (Romans 1:16).

The Simplicity of the Gospel

As we study the strange manipulations of men in the things of God, we can only shake our heads and wonder what a mess some of them have made of the gospel. The apostle Paul commented:

> I hope you will put up with a little of my foolishness; but you are already doing that. I am jealous for you with a godly jealousy. I promised you to one husband, to Christ, so that I might present you as a pure virgin to him. But I am afraid that just as Eve was deceived by the serpent's cunning, your minds may somehow be led astray from your sincere and pure devotion to Christ. For if someone comes to you and preaches a Jesus other than the Jesus we preached, or if you receive a different spirit from the one you received, or a different gospel from the one you accepted, you put up with it easily enough (2 Corinthians 11:1-4).

The key here is *the simplicity of the gospel*. The Bible is not obtuse; it gives us a clear, simple picture of the truth.

The aberrant religious groups cloud the clarity of the Word and bring chaos to the soul. Let's look at the simplicity of the gospel for a moment.

What God's Word Says

1. There is only one true God (Deuteronomy 6:4; Isaiah 43:10,11; 1 Corinthians 8:4).

2. God is a Spirit who fills the heavens and the earth (Jeremiah 23:24; John 4:24).

3. God is not a man (Numbers 23:19; Job 9:32; Hosea 11:9).

4. Jesus is Almighty God manifest in the flesh (John 1:1-3,14,18; Colossians 1:15-17; 1 Timothy 3:16).

5. Jesus preexisted in heaven. Man didn't (John 8:23; 1 Corinthians 15:46-49; Genesis 2:7; Zechariah 12:1).

6. We become children of God by adoption (Romans 8:14-16; Galatians 4:5,6; Ephesians 1:5).

7. The gospel (good news) by which we are saved is that Jesus provided forgiveness of sins, resurrection, and eternal life through His finished work (1 Corinthians 15:1-4; Hebrews 1:3; John 19:30; Colossians 1:20-22).

8. We are saved by grace through faith unto good works as God's workmanship (Ephesians 2:8-10).

9. God makes us new creatures as the Author and Finisher of our faith (2 Corinthians 5:17-21; Hebrews 12:2).

So, what must one do to be saved?

1. Confess your sins to God and turn from them (Romans 3:23; 1 John 1:8,9).

2. Confess with your mouth the Lord Jesus and believe with your heart that God raised Him from the dead (Romans 10:9).

3. Ask Jesus to come into your life and make you what He wants you to be (Philippians 2:13; 3:9; Romans 12:1,2).

1

Fast Facts on

Atheism

I t is philosophically impossible to be an atheist, since to be an atheist you must have infinite knowledge in order to know absolutely that there is no God. But to have infinite knowledge, you would have to be God yourself. It's hard to be God yourself and an atheist at the same time! The Bible says in Psalm 14:1, "The fool says in his heart, 'There is no God.'"

The apostle Paul says in Romans 1:18-23,25:

> The wrath of God is being revealed from heaven against all the godlessness and wickedness of men who suppress the truth [of God] by their wickedness, since what may be known about God is plain to them, because God has made it plain to them. For since the creation of the world God's invisible qualities—his eternal power and divine nature—have been clearly seen, being understood from what has been made, so that men are without excuse.
>
> For although they knew God, they neither glorified him as God nor gave thanks to him, but their thinking became futile and their foolish hearts were darkened. Although they claimed to be wise, they became fools and exchanged the glory of the immortal God for images made to look like mortal man, and birds and animals and reptiles. . . .
>
> They exchanged the truth of God for a lie, and worshiped and served created things rather than the Creator—who is forever praised.

God has clearly revealed himself in four major ways, so that man is without excuse when it comes to the knowledge of God.

Revealed Through Creation

First, God has revealed Himself to us through what He has created. The Bible begins with the words "In the beginning God created the heavens and the earth." Psalm 19:1 says, "The heavens declare the glory of God; the skies proclaim the work of his hands."

While Ron was speaking at a university on the scientific evidence for creation, a student of physics said to him, "I don't care what you say, I'm still going to believe in evolution!" Ron pulled up his shirtsleeve and showed him his wristwatch. Ron said, "You see this watch? I went down to a junkyard and found some rusty, twisted pieces of metal and threw them into a shoebox and began to shake it. I shook it for two weeks, two months, six months, twelve months, and all of a sudden, "bang!" It began to tick off 60 seconds a minute, 60 minutes an hour, 24 hours a day; it tells the day and date all by chance. Amazing!"

The student laughed and said, "That's impossible!" Ron replied, "You mean to tell me that this watch being created by chance is impossible, yet you tell me that my eyes, which see in 3-D and color, or my brain, which has 120 billion cells and 130 trillion electronic/chemical connections, are just a product of chance?"

We submit to you that it takes far more faith to believe in impersonal chance evolution than it does to believe in a divine Designer, who designed and created this incredible and intricate world we live in.

The Desire to Know God

We also know there is a God because God has put into the heart of every person a desire to know Him. Romans 1:18-25 makes clear that all people have an innate knowledge of God, but many have turned their backs to this knowledge and have rejected the revelation of God to follow *other gods*.

The fallacy of atheism is shown in the fact that when people declare "There is no God," instead of worshiping nothing, they always find something to worship. Man has a spiritual desire for God which he will fill either with the true God or with false gods. This is universally observable, whether it is the wooden idols of primitive societies or the gods of success, money, and material possessions of so-called sophisticated civilizations.

God in Human History

We also know there is a God because God has broken into human history. God split history into B.C. and A.D. and has personally revealed Himself to us. "History" is literally "His story."

Ron has had the privilege as a lecturer of traveling and speaking in over 75 countries of the world on six continents. One illustration that he uses is easily understood around the world in every culture. He tells the story of a father and son walking down a dirt path one day. They come upon an anthill that had been recently stepped on by another person in front of them. The little boy, who was only five years old, looked up to his daddy and said, "Daddy, wouldn't it be great if we could go down and tell those ants we love them! Tell those ants we care about them and help them with their sick and wounded!"

The father put his arm around his son and said, "Son, the only way we could tell those ants that we love them, that we care for them, and that we want to help them with their sick and wounded would be to become an ant! We would have to live like an ant and talk like an ant, and then by our lives they would know what we are like!"

Two thousand years ago, God looked down on a world that He had created and that He loved. He said, "I want to tell you how much I love you!" How was God going to do this? God said, "I will become a man. I will live like a man and talk like a man, and by my life they will know what I am like!" Two thousand years ago, the greatest event in human history took place: God became a man. His name was Jesus Christ! If you want to know what God is like, look at Jesus

Christ. The Bible says in Colossians 1:15 that He is the visible image of the invisible God.

Jesus Christ is the "television set of God." Right now as you read these words, there are actual television waves bouncing all around you! You cannot see them or hear them, but they are there. They are invisible, yet real. If you take a box called a television set and turn it on next to you, those invisible waves will become visible. You will see a picture and hear sound.

Two thousand years ago, God, who is invisible Spirit (John 4:24), became visible in the person of Jesus Christ! God the Creator of the universe took on human flesh and became a man so that we could both know what He is like and know Him personally. The greatest truth of history is that God has personally revealed Himself to us. He did not leave us alone in the universe, but has personally communicated to us, His creation!

Revealed in the Book

God has also revealed Himself to us through His Word, the Bible. Second Timothy 3:16 says, "All Scripture is God-breathed." Second Peter 1:21 says, "Men spoke from God as they were carried along by the Holy Spirit." The Bible has been translated into over 1800 languages and is consistently the number one bestseller every year for a very good reason: It is recognized as a supernatural book, divinely inspired by the Creator and Redeemer of the universe. The supernatural imprint of God is evident to anyone who will truly examine this remarkable Book.

First is the incredible unity and harmony of what is more than just one book. The Bible is actually the collection of 66 different books written by 40 different authors over a period of 1500 years. Yet we find that from Genesis to Revelation, God has given us a revelation of Himself and His desire for mankind that is a perfect unity and harmony. We challenge anyone who does not believe the Bible to be a supernatural book to bring together any other 66 books of your choosing which were written by 40 different authors over 1500 years and find the consistency and unity of theme and purpose that you have in the Holy Bible.

The Bible's integrity is also verified by its historical, geographical, and archaeological accuracy. One of the truly awe-inspiring evidences that it is God's Book is demonstrated by the hundreds of fulfilled prophecies given through the inspired prophets.

The Bible is God's love letter to you. God has taken the initiative to tell you that He loves you and wants to have a personal relationship with you! The message of the Bible and God's revelation to mankind is summed up in the best-known verses of the Bible, John 3:16,17:

> For God so loved the world that He gave His only begotten Son, that whoever believes in Him should not perish but have everlasting life. For God did not send His Son into the world to judge the world, but that the world through Him might be saved (NKJV).

Atheism is not a valid philosophy. It is intellectually bankrupt and demonstrates a willful denial of all that God has revealed. It is the very denial of the world around us and all the stars in the heavens.

2

Fast Facts on

Buddhism

Buddha means "the Enlightened One." Siddhartha Gautama, who most probably lived
from 563 to 483 B.C., was born into a wealthy Hindu family.
He lived a sheltered early life in the hill country bordering
modern-day India and Nepal. After marriage and the birth
of a son, he ventured out one day and saw the suffering of
the world. The sight of those who were suffering, sick, and
dying had such a profound impact on him that he left his
wife and son and set out on a life as an ascetic. Siddhartha's
goal was to find a release from this world of suffering and
pain. After six years, having been reduced to skin and
bones, he sat down under the bo tree near the river Gaya.
Here, during meditation, he achieved "Enlightenment"
and became the Buddha, or "Enlightened one."

In 1988, Ron personally visited Sarnath, six miles north
of Varanasi (Benares) and the Ganges River in northern
India. It was here that Buddha preached his first sermon
and gained his first following of Buddhist monks. Buddha's
teaching (or dharma) proclaimed the "Four Noble Truths"
that he discovered through "Enlightenment."

The Basics of Buddhism

The "Four Noble Truths" that form the foundation of
Buddhism are:

1) Life is suffering.

2) Suffering is caused by desire.

3) The cessation of desire eliminates suffering.

4) The stopping of desire comes by following "The Middle Way" between the extremes of sensuousness and asceticism.

This "Middle Way" that Buddha taught was achieved through the "Eightfold Path" that combined the knowledge of the Four Noble Truths with morality and meditation. The "Eightfold Path" encompasses the following "Right" things:

1) Right View.

2) Right Resolve.

3) Right Speech.

4) Right Action.

5) Right Livelihood.

6) Right Effort.

7) Right Concentration.

8) Right Ecstasy.

Right View is having an understanding of the Four Noble Truths listed above. Right Resolve is the decision to follow and observe them. Right Speech, Action, and Livelihood are the practical actions to avoid the desires of this life which produce suffering.

The last three steps of the Eightfold Path are more spiritual in their concern. Right Effort is the emptying of the mind, directing your attention toward final liberation from the world of suffering. Right Concentration involves the higher states of mind and body control.

Right Ecstasy is achieved when all the sense experiences cease and universal knowledge is obtained. This is release or final liberation, where you are no longer reborn through reincarnation. You become one with the Impersonal, the state of Nirvana. It is often described as the blowing out of a candle. You lose all personality and awareness and merge into "nothingness." At this point, Buddha said, you will be at peace. But it is always at the loss of your own soul and personality.

The goal of human existence, Buddha taught, was to free oneself from the law of "Karma" (cause and effect of good and bad deeds) and achieve the state of "Nirvana," where one ceases desiring and thus eliminates suffering.

The Two Main Branches

Today, Buddhism is divided into two main branches. One is Theravada or "Little Vehicle" and the other is Mahayana, the "Great Vehicle." The term "Vehicle" represents for Buddhists the belief that Buddhist doctrine is a vehicle or ship taking them through this life of suffering to a "beyond" or state of bliss, known as Nirvana.

The earliest form of Buddhism was Theravada, the concept that salvation was limited to Monks alone. This is found today largely in the countries of Thailand, Burma, Sri Lanka, Laos, and Cambodia. Today, Mahayana Buddhism accounts for the vast majority of Buddhism and is found primarily in the countries of Nepal, Tibet, China, Japan, Korea, and Vietnam, and is now being accepted by many people in the West who are fascinated by the Orient and its religions. It teaches that salvation or Nirvana is open to all true seekers.

Yet Siddhartha Gautama Buddha was in fact a Hindu from birth. *He never intended to start a religion, but was seeking to reform Hinduism.* He felt that Hinduism had lost its true essence by the incorporation of thousands of gods, all represented by idols. Buddha was an atheist. He did not believe in God and felt that the very concept of God or gods was holding people bound to this physical world of karma and suffering. What is so interesting about all this is how idolatry, which Buddha condemned, has become such a major part of Buddhism, with its many shrines and statues of Buddha, the very one who loathed these things!

Having lectured throughout southeast Asia, Ron has personally visited many of these Buddhist shrines and has seen the thousands of Buddha idols that people now pray to. Ron and Ed visited such a shrine in the Philippines and all but wept at the futility of people bowing before dead statues. For these many people, Buddha has become their god.

In the hill country of Sri Lanka, where the majority of the world's blue sapphires are mined, Ron lectured several years ago in the city of Kandy. Kandy is the home of the famous Temple of the Tooth—which has a tooth of Buddha. Yes, Buddha's tooth! Here he watched as people brought flowers and rice as offerings and bowed down to worship and pray to a gold box encrusted with jewels. Once a year, in a large festival, they bring out the box, open it, and reveal the sacred tooth of the Buddha for all to worship.

The largest Buddhist pagoda in the world is in Rangoon, Burma. The Shwe Dagon or Golden Pagoda contains over 3500 idols of Buddha. Every day of the year, people parade up the winding steps of this 300-foot monument to place thin pieces of gold on the shrine, light candles and incense, and pray for their dead ancestors before these wood, stone, and metal statues.

The Sad End of Idolatry

The gross idolatry that Buddhism has become is the sad and logical end of a religion that has rejected the personal Creator of the universe.

> Professing to be wise, they became fools, and changed the glory of the incorruptible God into an image made like corruptible man—and birds and four-footed beasts and creeping things (Romans 1:22,23 NKJV).

> For the customs of the peoples are worthless; they cut a tree out of the forest, and a craftsman shapes it with his chisel. They adorn it with silver and gold; they fasten it with hammer and nails so it will not totter. Like a scarecrow in a melon patch, their idols cannot speak; they must be carried because they cannot walk. Do not fear them; they can do no harm nor can they do any good. No one is like you, O Lord; you are great, and your name is mighty in power. Who should not revere you, O King of the nations? This is your due. Among all the wise men of the nations and in all their kingdoms, there is no one

like you. They are all senseless and foolish; they are taught by worthless wooden idols.

Hammered silver is brought from Tarshish and gold from Uphaz. What the craftsman and goldsmith have made is then dressed in blue and purple—all made by skilled workers. But the Lord is the true God; he is the living God, the eternal King. When he is angry, the earth trembles; the nations cannot endure his wrath. Tell them this: "These gods, who did not make the heavens and the earth, will perish from the earth and from under the heavens."

But God made the earth by his power; he founded the world by his wisdom and stretched out the heavens by his understanding. When he thunders, the waters in the heavens roar; he makes clouds rise from the ends of the earth. He sends lightning with the rain and brings out the wind from his storehouses. Everyone is senseless and without knowledge; every goldsmith is shamed by his idols. His images are a fraud; they have no breath in them. They are worthless, the objects of mockery; when their judgment comes, they will perish (Jeremiah 10:3-15).

Reaching Out with the Truth

As Christians we must reach out to the Buddhist with the truth of the gospel presented in love. The apostle Paul had a similar experience with the people of Athens who had also turned to idols in their search for truth. His defense of the faith is recorded for us in Acts chapter 17.

> While Paul was waiting for them in Athens, he was greatly distressed to see that the city was full of idols. So he reasoned in the synagogue with the Jews and the God-fearing Greeks, as well as in the marketplace day by day with those who happened to be there (Acts 17:16,17).

> Then they took him and brought him to a meeting of the Areopagus, where they said to him, "May

we know what this new teaching is that you are presenting? You are bringing some strange ideas to our
ears, and we want to know what they mean" (Acts
17:19,20).

Paul then stood up in the meeting of the Areopagus
and said: "Men of Athens! I see that in every way you
are very religious. For as I walked around and observed your objects of worship, I even found an altar
with this inscription: TO AN UNKNOWN GOD. Now
what you worship as something unknown I am going
to proclaim to you. The God who made the world and
everything in it is the Lord of heaven and earth and
does not live in temples built by hands. And he is not
served by human hands, as if he needed anything,
because he himself gives all men life and breath and
everything else" (Acts 17:22-25).

"Therefore since we are God's offspring, we should
not think that the divine being is like gold or silver or
stone—an image made by man's design and skill. In
the past God overlooked such ignorance, but now he
commands all people everywhere to repent. For he
has set a day when he will judge the world with justice
by the man he has appointed. He has given proof of
this to all men by raising him from the dead" (Acts
17:29-31).

Who Really Cares?

While speaking in Thailand, Ron was invited to visit
some of the refugee camps along the Cambodian border.
Over 300,000 refugees were caught in a no-man's-land
along the border. This resulted from the Cambodian mas-
sacre under Pol Pot and the Khmer Rouge in the mid-70's
(which came to be known as the "killing fields") and then
subsequently by the invasion of the Vietnamese at the end
of the 70's.

One of the most fascinating things about these refugee
camps was the realization of who was caring for the refugees. Here, in this Buddhist country of Thailand, with

Buddhist refugees coming from Cambodia and Laos, there were no Buddhists taking care of their Buddhist brothers. There were also no Hindus or Muslims taking care of those people. The only people there, taking care of these 300,000 people, were Christians from Christian mission organizations and Christian relief organizations!

One of the men Ron was with had lived in Thailand for over 20 years and was heading up a major portion of the relief effort for one of these organizations. He asked him, "Why, in a Buddhist country, with Buddhist refugees, are there no Buddhists here taking care of their Buddhist brothers?" Ron will never forget his answer: "Ron, have you ever seen what Buddhism does to a nation or a people? Buddha taught that each man is an island unto himself. Buddha said, 'If someone is suffering, that is his karma.' You are not to interfere with another person's karma because he is purging himself through suffering and reincarnation! Buddha said, 'You are to be an island unto yourself.'"

This leader of the relief effort continued, "Ron, the only people that have a reason to be here today taking care of these 300,000 refugees are Christians. It is only in Christianity that people have a basis for human value, that people are important enough to educate and to care for. For Christians, these people are of ultimate value, created in the image of God, so valuable that Jesus Christ died for each and every one of them. You find *that* value in no other religion, in no other philosophy, but in Jesus Christ!"

The True Difference

In his freshman year in college, Ron lived next door in the dorm to a student from Thailand. He had been raised a Buddhist, in a Buddhist family. At the age of 18 he had heard the claims of Jesus Christ from a missionary and had responded by receiving Jesus Christ as Lord and Savior. Ron asked him one day, "Why did you become a Christian? What is the difference between Buddhism and Christianity?"

He replied, "Ron, when I was a Buddhist, it was like I was drowning in a big lake and I didn't know how to swim.

I was going under for the third time when Buddha walked up to the edge of the lake and began to teach me how to swim. Buddha said, 'Start moving your hands and kicking your legs, but you have to make it to shore yourself!' Then Jesus Christ walked up to the edge of the lake, but He did not stop there! He dove into the lake, swam out, rescued me, and brought me to shore. After He brought me to shore, then He taught me how to swim, so I could go back and rescue others!"

This is the difference between Buddhism and Christianity. This is the difference between the religions of man and Christianity. Christianity is not a religion! Religion is man's attempt to reach God. Religion is man trying to get to God through his rituals, sacrifices, traditions, or good works. But the Bible says that "all our righteous acts are like filthy rags" before a holy God (Isaiah 64:6). God is holy and man is affected with a spiritual disease called sin: "For all have sinned and fall short of the glory of God" (Romans 3:23). Man is incapable of coming into the presence of a holy God through the doorway of religion. This is the great truth of Christianity. Romans 5:8 says, "But God demonstrates his own love for us in this: While we were still sinners, Christ died for us."

Religion is man trying to get to God, but Christianity is God reaching down to man. God took the initiative and sent Jesus Christ into the world to take our sin that separated us from God, and to nail that sin onto a cross. He then covered that sin with His blood as the payment to restore us back into full relationship with Himself.

This is why it is called the "gospel" or "good news." It is very good news to people caught up in man-made religions that enslave them to rituals and traditions that can save no one. Buddhism, with its denial of God and teaching of Karma, fails to respond to the basic fact that *man is a sinner in need of a Savior.* Man cannot save himself no matter how many "Noble Truths" he thinks up, no matter how at peace he lives. There is only one truth that will truly set people free. Jesus said, *"I am the way and the truth and the life. No one comes to the Father except through me* (John 14:6).

3

The Character of God

We talk a lot about God. Some of it is good talk and some of it isn't. Sometimes the way we use the name of God is not just disrespectful but downright blasphemous. The Greeks declared that the greatest activity of man was to think. From the Christian perspective, the greatest thinking anyone could do is to think about God. That is the greatest activity of man.

As we begin to study the things that people *incorrectly* say to God and about God, we need to think about the true nature and character of God. It is very important that we spend some time here, because this is where the cults step away from sound doctrine and go off on their many tangents from the truth. Most of them break down on the doctrine of God.

A.W. Tozer said in his classic work *The Knowledge of the Holy*, "Worship is pure or base as one entertains high or low thoughts of God." He also said that "we tend, by some secret law of the soul, to move toward our mental image of God." What you think about God will directly affect how you live as well as how you worship. The sad thing is that too many people have too small a concept of God, an inadequate view of God.

Tozer continued, "An inadequate view of God is actually idolatry. To worship God or to worship anything less than what God has revealed Himself to be is idolatry." And this fits what we have seen throughout the world: Millions of people bowing before little stone images of their gods.

Were we to make a statue of Buddha that was a hundred times the size of the largest Buddha in the world, it would still be a little idol compared to the God who created the whole universe.

God from Man's Viewpoint

There are many humanists and philosophers today who seek to study God from man's viewpoint. We have the study of the *philosophy* of religion, the *sociology* of religion, the *anthropology* of religion, and the *psychology* of religion. Man, beginning with the image of himself as the model, seeks to define what God is like. But man, beginning from himself, can only arrive at a very small and warped concept of God.

This is where we end up in many of our aberrational theologies, such as pantheism, deism, and a variety of other concepts. J.B. Phillips wrote the book *Your God Is Too Small* because he felt that too many people have an entirely inadequate view of God. The reasonable question to ask is "What has God revealed to us about Himself?"

If we look at it merely from man's viewpoint we will run into the danger that C.S. Lewis, the late professor at Oxford and Cambridge Universities, talked about. Lewis told the story of a wise barnacle that was sitting down at the bottom of the ocean attached to his rock. One day, in a moment of mystical enlightenment, he got a glimpse of what man was like. So he gathered around him his barnacle disciples and began to expound upon the nature of man. He said, "Man has no shell, man is not attached to a rock, and man is not surrounded by water."

As time went on, a few of the barnacles got some idea of what man was like. They soon began to rationalize that, since man had no shell, he must be a shapeless blob of jelly. Since man was not attached to a rock, it was quite obvious that he had no location where he lived. And since man was not surrounded by water, as they were, it was reasonable to assume that man did not eat, since he had nothing to float food to him.

The barnacles therefore concluded that man was far less active and important than barnacles were. From their viewpoint, from their environment and nature, they had extrapolated an extremely limited and warped concept of man.

We have the same danger as the barnacles if we begin with ourselves, limited to a finite, three-dimensional, naturalistic worldview. If we use this basis it is most probable that we too, like many of the cults today, will end up with an extremely limited and warped concept of God, one which is far less than who He really is.

Just as the barnacles could never know what man was like unless man chose to break into their environment and personally reveal himself to the barnacles, so too man cannot know what God is like unless God chooses to personally reveal Himself to us. This is what God did, both in His inspired Word, the Bible, and through the incarnation, when God broke into human history and became a man.

What we must do in our study of God is to see *what God has revealed to us concerning His nature*. God has given us the Scriptures for one purpose: to reveal His nature and character to us. As we go through the Scriptures we see God revealing Himself to us. If we read the book of Jonah, we see God's universal love for mankind and His desire to bring mankind to a relationship with Him. In the book of Genesis, we read about God's creation and also about God's judgment. The book of Hosea tells us about God's overwhelming compassion and love for mankind. In the book of Amos, we read about God's righteousness. In Micah we read about God's justice. In Isaiah we read about His holiness and His redemptive love. In the book of John, we discover that God loved us so much that He sent His only begotten Son to die for us, to redeem us from the curse of sin. As we go throughout the Scriptures, *God reveals to us who He is and how we can know Him*.

Now let's look briefly at God's personal revelation to us concerning His nature, so that we might have an accurate concept of what God is like. Rather than worshiping something less than who God really is, we can then lift up God as He has revealed Himself in Scripture.

God Is Spirit

We first discover that the Bible declares that God is spirit with life and personality. Jesus tells us in John 4:24 that "God is spirit." Now the logical question is "What is a spirit?" In Luke 24:37-39, after Jesus was raised from the dead, His astonished disciples thought He was a spirit. Jesus told them, "Look at my hands and my feet. It is I myself! Touch me and see; a ghost [spirit] does not have flesh and bones, as you see I have." When He asked His disciples who they thought He was, He again opened a window so they could see the true nature of God.

> "But what about you?" he asked. "Who do you say I am?" Simon Peter answered, "You are the Christ, the Son of the living God." Jesus replied, "Blessed are you, Simon son of Jonah, for this was not revealed to you by man, but by my Father in heaven" (Matthew 16:15-17).

This is not something that man had to wait for until New Testament days to discover about God. In Deuteronomy 4:12 we find this: "Then the Lord spoke to you out of the fire. You heard the sound of words but saw no form; there was only a voice." They heard the sound of words, but saw no form—only a voice.

God's declaration of Himself and His very nature continues in verse 15:

> You saw no form of any kind the day the Lord spoke to you at Horeb out of the fire. Therefore watch yourselves very carefully.

The Word continues with God's warning to any who would corrupt His very nature:

> . . . so that you do not become corrupt and make for yourselves an idol, an image of any shape, whether formed like a man or a woman, or like any animal on earth or any bird that flies in the air, or like any creature that moves along the ground or any fish in the

waters below. And when you look up to the sky and
see the sun, the moon and the stars—all the heavenly
array—do not be enticed into bowing down to them
and worshiping things the Lord your God has appor-
tioned to all the nations under heaven (Deuteronomy
4:16-19).

God spoke to Moses out of the fire; Moses heard only a
voice. There was no man standing there in the flames, but
God, who says He is spirit, was there.

God Is Living

The Scriptures tell us that God is not only a spirit, but
that He is a spirit with life and personality. He is a *living*
God, not merely an impersonal force. Jeremiah 10 is one of
the greatest chapters in the Bible dealing with the nature of
God. Here we see the distinction between idols made with
the hands of man and the living God.

No one is like you, O Lord; you are great, and your
name is mighty in power. Who should not revere you,
O King of the nations? This is your due. Among all the
wise men of the nations and in all their kingdoms,
there is no one like you. They are all senseless and
foolish; they are taught by worthless wooden idols.
Hammered silver is brought from Tarshish and gold
from Uphaz. What the craftsman and goldsmith have
made is then dressed in blue and purple—all made by
skilled workers. But the Lord is the true God; he is the
living God, the eternal King. When he is angry, the
earth trembles; the nations cannot endure his wrath.
Tell them this: "These gods, who did not make the
heavens and the earth, will perish from the earth and
from under the heavens." But God made the earth by
his power; he founded the world by his wisdom and
stretched out the heavens by his understanding. When
he thunders, the waters in the heavens roar; he makes
clouds rise from the ends of the earth. He sends lightning with the rain and brings out the wind from his
storehouses. Everyone is senseless and without knowledge; every goldsmith is shamed by his idols. His

images are a fraud; they have no breath in them. They are worthless, the objects of mockery; when their judgment comes, they will perish. He who is the Portion of Jacob is not like these, for he is the Maker of all things, including Israel, the tribe of his inheritance— the Lord Almighty is his name (Jeremiah 10:6-16).

There is no other god like our God! Verse 10 says it plainly: "The Lord is the true God; he is the living God, the eternal King."

He is not like those idols that cannot speak. No, He is a living God. God is spirit, with life and personality. He speaks, He hears, He sees, He declares, He creates, He wills. He expresses anger, remorse, joy. He loves, He judges. God is personal, He is a personal Creator, and He is personally concerned about each of us as His personal creations. *God is alive with life and personality.*

To say that God is devoid of these attributes is to make Him far less than who He really is. This is where many of the cults make their major mistake. Mary Baker Eddy taught in Christian Science that God is merely a divine principle. The same is true of the Unity School of Christianity; it says that God is merely an impersonal force. But a "divine principle" and an "impersonal force" never loved anybody. Only a *personality* can love. God, who created this world, can love *because* He is living and personal. It isn't something He learned to do. He always was God and He always had this nature.

God Is Self-Existent

The Bible declares that God is the self-existent One. He has always eternally existed. He has no beginning and no end. He alone was and is God. There were and are no others. As Isaiah 44:6 says, "I am the first and I am the last; apart from me there is no God."

Moses was told by God in Exodus 3:14: "This is what you are to say to the Israelites: 'I AM' has sent me to you.'" God was declaring that He was unique from man. You cannot label God or define Him the way you would a man. He is the eternal One.

This is a mistake that many philosophers and humanistic theologians have made, those who hold to a naturalistic system. They have set up a definition so small that God can't fit inside it. For example, many people are saying that the only reality today is what we find in our three-dimensional world of naturalism.

But God is far bigger than our finite three dimensions. He may be more than eight dimensions. He may be more than 100 dimensions. In fact, we don't have any idea how complex He really is. But He has broken into the narrow confines of our small box called Earth to communicate to us who He is. He is the self-existent One who alone has life in Himself.

The very first verse of the Bible tells us a little about the width and breadth of His life and power: "In the beginning God created the heavens and the earth." Acts 17:25 tells us that He is the giver of life to all things. In Colossians 1:16,17 we read:

> By him all things were created: things in heaven and on earth, visible and invisible, whether thrones or powers or rulers or authorities; all things were created by him and for him. He is before all things, and in him all things hold together.

God Is Immutable

We also discover that God, by His very nature, is immutable. By "immutability" we mean that God does not change. Malachi 3:6 tells us, "I the Lord do not change." Ecclesiastes 3:14 affirms that *everything* God does remains forever and that nothing can be added to it or taken from it. Hebrews 6:17,18 tells us that God is immutable. He does not change and He does not lie.

These are tremendous truths to understand because we are living in a world of constant change and turmoil. But we have a solid foundation, a solid rock, in God. He is the same yesterday, today, and forever. God does not change as to

His nature or purpose. He has never done so in the entire history of mankind and He will never do so through the end of time.

Many of the groups that we will discuss in this book have gods who change and vacillate. Their worshipers live on a seesaw of doubts and fear, manipulated by the holy priests of their faiths. They cannot conceive of the peace that comes from being at the altar of a never-changing, loving, caring God.

God, while never changing, may still use different methods with us. He dealt with Moses one way, He dealt with Noah in another way, and He dealt with Abraham in still another way. He may have dealt with you in one way and us in some other, but His purpose is the same and His nature remains the same. God is immutable, and because of this immutability God is always consistent in truth.

When God reveals something to us, He never contradicts Himself. It is because of His immutability that we can test all the latter-day revelations coming from all the false teachers of all the cults today: God does not change. It is almost humorous to see how quickly many of these latter-day prophets fall by the wayside when tested by God's Word.

Since God does not change, He is consistent in truth. He never communicates one truth to one generation and then a contradicting truth to a different generation. He is always consistent in truth. Simply put, truth is truth. How many times, when we were children, did we try to bend the yoke of truth at home or at school? It rarely worked with mom and the teacher, and it never will work with God!

Therefore, should God theoretically choose to give a *new* revelation today, it must be consistent with His oldest revelation, the written Word of God. If a revelation given by someone today contradicts the earliest revelation, then we immediately know it is not of God.

> Your Word, O Lord, is eternal; it stands firm in the heavens. Your faithfulness continues through all generations. . . . Your word is a lamp to my feet and a light for my path (Psalm 119:89,90,105).

Heaven and earth will pass away, but my words will never pass away (Matthew 24:35).

All Scripture is God-breathed and is useful for teaching, rebuking, correcting and training in righteousness, so that the man of God may be thoroughly equipped for every good work (2 Timothy 3:16,17).

The word of God is living and active. Sharper than any double-edged sword, it penetrates even to dividing soul and spirit, joints and marrow; it judges the thoughts and attitudes of the heart. Nothing in all creation is hidden from God's sight. Everything is uncovered and laid bare before the eyes of him to whom we must give account (Hebrews 4:12,13).

I warn everyone who hears the words of the prophecy of this book: If anyone adds anything to them, God will add to him the plagues described in this book. And if anyone takes words away from this book of prophecy, God will take away from him his share in the tree of life and in the holy city, which are described in this book (Revelation 22:18,19).

We must test all things by the Word of God, and hold fast to that which is good, as we are exhorted in 1 Thessalonians 5:21.

God Is Omnipotent

The Bible also declares that God is omnipotent or all-powerful. He told Abraham, "I am God Almighty; walk before me" (Genesis 17:1). Matthew 19:26 says that "with God all things are possible." Revelation 19:6 tells us, "Hallelujah! For our Lord God Almighty reigns." His name is written, "KING OF KINGS AND LORD OF LORDS" (verse 16). Isaiah 40 is an exciting chapter that gives the meaning of the omnipotent power of our God. Beginning with verse 12 we read:

Who has measured the waters in the hollow of his hand, or with the breadth of his hand marked off the heavens? Who has held the dust of the earth in a basket, or weighed the mountains on the scales and the hills in a balance? Who has understood the mind of the Lord, or instructed him as his counselor? Whom did the Lord consult to enlighten him, and who taught him the right way? Who was it that taught him knowledge or showed him the path of understanding?

Surely the nations are like a drop in a bucket; they are regarded as dust on the scales; he weighs the islands as though they were fine dust. Lebanon is not sufficient for altar fires, nor its animals enough for burnt offerings. Before him all the nations are as nothing; they are regarded by him as worthless and less than nothing. To whom, then, will you compare God? What image will you compare him to? As for an idol, a craftsman casts it, and a goldsmith overlays it with gold and fashions silver chains for it. A man too poor to present such an offering selects wood that will not rot. He looks for a skilled craftsman to set up an idol that will not topple.

Do you not know? Have you not heard? Has it not been told you from the beginning? Have you not understood since the earth was founded? He sits enthroned above the circle of the earth, and its people are like grasshoppers. He stretches out the heavens like a canopy, and spreads them out like a tent to live in. He brings princes to naught and reduces the rulers of this world to nothing. No sooner are they planted, no sooner are they sown, no sooner do they take root in the ground, than he blows on them and they wither, and a whirlwind sweeps them away like chaff. "To whom will you compare me? Or who is my equal?" says the Holy One. Lift your eyes and look to the heavens: Who created all these? He who brings out the starry host one by one, and calls them each by name. Because of his great power and mighty strength, not one of them is missing.

Why do you say, O Jacob, and complain, O Israel,

"My way is hidden from the Lord; my cause is disregarded by my God"? Do you not know? Have you not heard? The Lord is the everlasting God, the Creator of the ends of the earth. He will not grow tired or weary, and his understanding no one can fathom. He gives strength to the weary and increases the power of the weak. Even youths grow tired and weary, and young men stumble and fall; but those who hope in the Lord will renew their strength. They will soar on wings like eagles; they will run and not grow weary, they will walk and not be faint (Isaiah 40:12-31).

What a tremendous chapter! If you want to wake up and be inspired every morning, read Isaiah 40 and get a glimpse of what God is like. He holds the entire cosmos together by the power of His hand! He knows every star in the universe by its name, and every hair of your head. That's the God we worship.

Have you ever truly thought about how great God is? Have you ever imagined what the magnitude of the cosmos really is? The speed of light is 186,000 miles per second. In one second, light can travel around the earth at the equator 7½ times!

If you go outside on a clear night, you can see a band going across the sky which appears as dense clouds across the center of the sky. Actually that is the rim of what we earthlings call the Milky Way. What you are seeing are not clouds but stars, so many billions of stars that it appears to us to be clouds. If you were traveling at the speed of light, it would take you 4½ years just to reach the nearest star you can see at night!

A light-year is how far light travels in one year. In one year light will travel 6 trillion miles. The nearest star is Alpha Centauri, 4½ light-years away, which means that the nearest star that you can see at night is something like 27 trillion miles away! And that is just the *nearest* star in our galaxy. There are over 100 billion stars in our Milky Way galaxy!

As huge as this sounds, ours is one of the *smallest* galaxies in the universe! In fact, astronomers with the

200-inch telescope at Mount Palomar in California estimate that as they look out through the cup of the Big Dipper constellation they can see over one million galaxies the size of our Milky Way or bigger!

At the speed of light it would take us a hundred thousand light-years to cross the Milky Way galaxy. This means that our small galaxy is six hundred thousand trillion miles across. And astronomers can see over one million galaxies that size or bigger *just in the cup of the big dipper. Think of the magnitude of what we are saying!*

Leaving the Milky Way galaxy, the farthest thing that astronomers can see or hear with their most sophisticated equipment is a quasar, which is 15 billion light-years away, which means it is 90 billion trillion miles away.

We have no idea what is beyond that, but astronomers estimate that this quasar 90 billion trillion miles away emits enough energy in one second to supply all the electrical needs of the earth for one million years. That's just *one* quasar, and there are *millions* of quasars in the universe. Do you begin to get the picture? The Bible says that the God who created all this holds it together *by the power of His hand.* And some people wonder if God is really big enough to solve their problems?

God is far bigger than our finite minds can hope to comprehend. Yet the God whose energy transcends all the energy in the universe by infinity nevertheless loves each one of us. That God is concerned about you personally.

The Bible says that God considers you more important than all those galaxies put together. What a tremendous truth! As you begin to get a glimpse of what God is really like, it will change the way you pray. When you come into the presence of the Almighty Creator, it becomes an awe-inspiring thing. It becomes a thing of *wonderment.*

God Is Omnipresent

Not only is God omnipotent, but He is also omnipresent. His omnipresence means that God is everywhere at once. From the farthest corner of the most distant galaxy to the deepest part of your heart, God is there. Listen to the rejoicing over God's omnipresence in Psalm 139, beginning with verse 5:

> You hem me in—behind and before; you have laid your hand upon me. Such knowledge is too wonderful for me, too lofty for me to attain.
>
> Where can I go from your Spirit? Where can I flee from your presence? If I go up to the heavens, you are there; if I make my bed in the depths, you are there. If I rise on the wings of the dawn, if I settle on the far side of the sea, even there your hand will guide me, your right hand will hold me fast.
>
> If I say, "Surely the darkness will hide me and the light become night around me," even the darkness will not be dark to you; the night will shine like the day, for darkness is as light to you. For you created my inmost being; you knit me together in my mother's womb.
>
> I praise you because I am fearfully and wonderfully made; your works are wonderful, I know that full well. My frame was not hidden from you when I was made in the secret place. When I was woven together in the depths of the earth, your eyes saw my unformed body. All the days ordained for me were written in your book before one of them came to be. How precious to me are your thoughts, O God! How vast is the sum of them! Were I to count them, they would outnumber the grains of sand. When I awake, I am still with you (Psalm 139:5-18).

Have you ever gone down to the ocean and tried to count the grains of sand on just one beach? God says He thinks about you continually and that the sum of His thoughts outnumber the grains of sand on the earth!

God Is Omniscient

We also refer to the omniscience of God, that fact that God is all-knowing.

> O Lord, you have searched me and you know me. You know when I sit and when I rise; you perceive my

thoughts from afar. You discern my going out and my lying down; you are familiar with all my ways. Before a word is on my tongue you know it completely, O Lord (Psalm 139:1-4).

The Lord searches every heart and understands every motive behind the thoughts (1 Chronicles 28:9).

He determines the number of the stars and calls them each by name. Great is our Lord and mighty in power; his understanding has no limit (Psalm 147:4,5).

Oh, the depth of the riches of the wisdom and knowledge of God! How unsearchable his judgments, and his paths beyond tracing out! (Romans 11:33).

Because God knows all things perfectly, He knows nothing better than any other thing, but all things equally well. God knows you and is concerned about you personally.

God Is Transcendent

Four attributes of God that help us avoid common fallacies are God's transcendence, His immanence, His immensity, and His eternity.

Transcendence means that God is detached from all His creation as an independent, self-existing being (Isaiah 40:12-17). God is not the creation or part of the creation. He is in fact the *Creator*, who created everything apart from Himself. This is why the Eastern concept of pantheism is not true. This is also why the New Age teaching of "Mother Earth" is not valid. God is not the earth or the cosmos. He is the *Creator*, not the creation!

Immanence means God's all-pervading presence and power within His creation. As Isaiah 57:15 says, "This is what the high and lofty One says—he who lives forever, whose name is holy: 'I live in a high and holy place, but also with him who is contrite and lowly in spirit, to revive the spirit of the lowly and to revive the heart of the contrite.'" God is actively concerned and involved with His creation. This attribute refutes the concept of deism, which says God wound up the world like a watch and then left it to run down on its own.

Immensity means that God is not confined by space. The fact that God is *eternal* means that He is not confined by time. Time and space are aspects of the created world. God by definition is outside time and space; He is not limited by our naturalistic, three-dimensional world, nor is He limited by the fourth dimension of time. God is supernatural, beyond our natural understanding. Isaiah 55:9 says, "As the heavens are higher than the earth, so are my ways higher than your ways and my thoughts than your thoughts."

God Is Sovereign

The Bible also speaks of God's sovereignty, the fact that He alone is the supreme authority, the only God, Creator, and Ruler in the universe.

> Yours, O Lord, is the greatness and the power and the glory and the majesty and the splendor, for everything in heaven and earth is yours. Yours, O Lord, is the kingdom; you are exalted as head over all. Wealth and honor come from you; you are the ruler of all things. In your hands are strength and power to exalt and give strength to all. Now, our God, we give you thanks, and praise your glorious name (1 Chronicles 29:11-13).

Isaiah 45:5,6 tells us:

> I am the Lord, and there is no other; apart from me there is no God. I will strengthen you, though you have not acknowledged me, so that from the rising of the sun to the place of its setting men may know there is none besides me. I am the Lord, and there is no other.

He alone is God. Before him there was no God and therefore there will be none after Him. Colossians 1:16 tells us that "all things were created by him and for him." First Timothy 6:15 tells us that God is "the blessed and only

Ruler, the King of kings and Lord of lords." Revelation 4:11 says:

> You are worthy, our Lord and God, to receive glory
> and honor and power, for you created all things, and
> by your will they were created and have their being.

He is the Sovereign Creator, He alone is God, and He alone is Lord.

God Is Holy

Now we come to a third area: the moral attributes of God. The basis of His moral attributes is His holiness. We are referring to God's absolute purity, perfection, and majesty.

Out of His holiness come three areas: His righteousness, His truth, and His love. Isaiah 6:3 tells us, "Holy, holy, holy is the Lord Almighty; the whole earth is full of his glory." Isaiah 57:15 tells us His name is holy; He dwells in the high and holy place. In Hosea 11:9 He tells us:

> I will not carry out my fierce anger, nor will I turn
> and devastate Ephraim. For I am God, and not man—
> the Holy One among you. I will not come in wrath.

God is holy and because of His holiness He demands righteousness. When we speak of His righteousness, we speak of three things: His mandatory righteousness, His punitive righteousness, and His redemptive righteousness. God demands righteousness because His holiness is our standard for living. In Leviticus 19:2 He says:

> Speak to the entire assembly of Israel and say to
> them: "Be holy because I, the Lord your God, am
> holy."

In 1 Peter 1:15,16 we read:

> Just as he who called you is holy, so be holy in all
> you do; for it is written: "Be holy, because I am holy."

What does God require? How are we to approach Him in His holiness and in our sin? In Micah 6:6-8, there is an answer.

> With what shall I come before the Lord and bow down before the exalted God? Shall I come before him with burnt offerings, with calves a year old? Will the Lord be pleased with thousands of rams, with ten thousand rivers of oil? Shall I offer my firstborn for my transgression, the fruit of my body for the sin of my soul? He has showed you, O man, what is good. And what does the Lord require of you? To act justly and to love mercy and to walk humbly with your God.

This is what God requires. He does not want our sacrifices or our burnt offerings. What God demands is justice, lovingkindness, and a humble walk with Him. God is intensely concerned with the *heart* of man. He is concerned with our attitude of life, that we grow in maturity in Jesus Christ so that we might become more like Him. He has given us the standard to be holy as He is holy. One day God will perfect us in holiness, but daily we are to grow in maturity and grow *toward* God's holiness to conform to His nature.

Psalm 96:13 tells us that one day God will judge the world in righteousness. Acts 17:30,31 repeats that concept:

> In the past God overlooked such ignorance, but now he commands all people everywhere to repent. For he has set a day when he will judge the world with justice by the man he has appointed. He has given proof of this to all men by raising him from the dead.

God Is Love

While His righteousness demands justice, God did not leave us to stand before the judgment seat uncovered in our sin. God does not merely parcel out justice, but He offers fallen man *redemption*. This is God's redemptive righteousness, a holiness which desires the redemption of mankind. Psalm 51 tells us that God is ready to restore salvation to us when we seek forgiveness with a contrite heart. Romans 3:23-26 tells us:

> All have sinned and fall short of the glory of God, and are justified freely by his grace through the redemption that came by Christ Jesus. God presented him as a sacrifice of atonement, through faith in his blood. He did this to demonstrate his justice, because in his forbearance he had left the sins committed beforehand unpunished—he did it to demonstrate his justice at the present time, so as to be just and the one who justifies those who have faith in Jesus.

In 2 Corinthians 5:17-21 we have this glorious promise:

> Therefore, if anyone is in Christ, he is a new creation; the old has gone, the new has come! All this is from God, who reconciled us to himself through Christ and gave us the ministry of reconciliation: that God was reconciling the world to himself in Christ, not counting men's sins against them. And he has committed to us the message of reconciliation.
>
> We are therefore Christ's ambassadors, as though God were making his appeal through us. We implore you on Christ's behalf: Be reconciled to God. God made him who had no sin to be sin for us, so that in him we might become the righteousness of God.

This brings us to our last points about the love of God and the truth of God. John 3:16 says:

> For God so loved the world that he gave his one and only Son, that whoever believes in him shall not perish but have eternal life.

This eternal life is not something that is out there somewhere in the future. The eternal life mentioned here starts *the moment one believes in Christ*. It is not only for eternity but is a qualitative life right now.

Psalm 103:17 says that God's lovingkindness is everlasting. John adds:

This is how God showed his love among us: He sent his one and only Son into the world that we might live through him. This is love: not that we loved God, but that he loved us and sent his Son as an atoning sacrifice for our sins (1 John 4:9,10).

Jesus was that infinite sacrifice. There needed to be that spotless Lamb of God who would take away the sins of the world.

Covered by Christ

When Ron was lecturing in New Zealand and Australia recently, the sheep ranchers told him what often happens in a large flock of sheep. When the mother ewes are giving birth to lambs there will often be a mother that dies while giving birth to a live lamb. But somewhere else in the flock a mother ewe gives birth to a dead lamb. The sheep ranchers bring the orphan lamb to the mother who lost her baby, in order for the orphan to nurse and feed. But the mother ewe can smell that it is not her baby, and she will always kick it away and not allow it to suckle. But the sheep ranchers have discovered that they can take the blood of the stillborn lamb and smear it as a covering over the fleece of the orphan lamb. Then when they bring that lamb to the mother who lost her baby, she will smell the blood, sense that it is her lamb, and allow it to nurse and feed.

It's the same way with God. God is holy and will not look upon our sin. But when the blood of Jesus Christ covers us and cleanses us and forgives us, the holy God looks down upon us and does not see our sinful nature. Instead, He sees the blood of Jesus Christ that covers us. So He accepts us as His own. It is the blood of Jesus Christ that covers us and cleanses us and reconciles us to a relationship with God.

You know that it was not with perishable things such as silver or gold that you were redeemed from the empty way of life handed down to you from your forefathers, but with the precious blood of Christ, a lamb without blemish or defect (1 Peter 1:18,19).

In him we have redemption through his blood, the forgiveness of sins, in accordance with the riches of God's grace (Ephesians 1:7).

God demonstrates his own love for us in this: While we were still sinners, Christ died for us. Since we have now been justified by his blood, how much more shall we be saved from God's wrath through him! (Romans 5:8,9).

God Is Truth

Finally, a word about the truth of God. Psalm 100:5 tells us that God's truth endures to all generations. Deuteronomy 32:4 says that God is a God of truth, and that His faithfulness remains forever. In John 8:31,32 we read:

To the Jews who had believed him, Jesus said, "If you hold to my teaching, you are really my disciples. Then you will know the truth, and the truth will set you free."

Jesus said He wants to make us free, and His truth will make us free: "If you abide in My word, you are My disciples indeed. And you shall know the truth, and the truth shall make you free" (NKJV). Christ, praying for those who called themselves His disciples, asked of the Father, *"Sanctify them by the truth; your word is truth"* (John 17:17).

God has given us a faithful and true revelation of His nature. As we go into the study of the false doctrines of man, we need to first look intently at the real God. Then we will never bow down and worship before something less than what God has revealed Himself to be.

4

Evolution: The Incredible Theory

One of the most important questions that anyone can ask today is regarding the question of origins. Today there are two competing philosophies on this issue. One is the theory of evolution, which says that men and women are merely an accident, evolved from slimy algae. The other view is Genesis 1:1, which says, "In the beginning God created...."

How you answer the question of origins, whether you are an accident or a unique creation of God, will ultimately determine everything else in your life. It will determine your value for human individuals, your basis of morality, your meaning and purpose in life, and your ultimate destiny. It is one of the most fundamental questions you can ask!

In this chapter we want to explore what evolution is and why it is one of the great falsehoods being perpetrated in our age. We also want to look at the scientific evidence and why it all points to the fact that you are not an accident, but a unique creation of an almighty loving Creator.

Lucky to Be Here?

The November 20, 1989, issue of *Newsweek* had an article expounding the modern theory of evolution. It was entitled "We're All Lucky to Be Here." Here is an excerpt:

> It is a picture we all carry around in our heads,

the most powerful icon of the of the Age of Secular Humanism: the line of ascent of Man. It begins with the bacteria, just barely across the threshold of life, a tenuous scum on the primeval seas. Then, climbing the ladder of complexity . . . protozoa, invertebrates, the fishes and early reptiles. Followed by the first mammals, which knocked off the dinosaurs, the early primates and their hominid descendants huddled around a cave fire. Three billion years of progress directed toward the production of Man.

. . . This view asserts that there is nothing inherent in the laws of nature that directed evolution toward the production of human beings. There is nothing predestined about our current preeminence among large terrestrial fauna; we are the product of a whole series of contingent events in the history of our planet, any one of which could have been reversed to give rise to a different outcome.

We are, in short, like every other creature that ever walked or slithered across the earth, an accident.

Time magazine had a cover story entitled "How Man Became Man" on November 7, 1977, in which this theme was given as the only plausible scientific reason for man being man. In that issue appeared an advertisement for the TIME/LIFE book series *The Emergence of Man*, which is now found in public schools and libraries throughout the United States. In the ad, the description of what you would learn included the following:

> . . . you share, with every other creature that ever lived, the same origins—the same accident that led to the spontaneous creation of the first single-celled algae 3.5 billion years ago.

Isn't that exciting to know! You all share the same accident and have evolved from the same algae billions of years ago. Now stop and think about this for a moment. Realize that this has become the basis of education throughout North America and most of the world today. We are raising a generation of young people to believe that there is no God and they are just accidents evolved from algae!

The Shaky Premise

If you are thinking at all, you have to ask yourselves some basic questions. What does this belief do to the value of human life and the basis of morality? If you teach people they are nothing but evolved animals, then why shouldn't they live like animals? Isn't the rise in violence just "survival of the fittest"? Aren't the out-of-wedlock teen pregnancies and the sexually transmitted diseases, including AIDS, the logical result of man living as an animal, with no basis for morals? Aren't the 30 million babies aborted in America since Roe v. Wade simply the end product of a philosophy that offers no value for human life? It may not be politically correct to say these things, but they are the truth!

The tragedy is that evolution is a nineteenth-century philosophy that has been destroyed by twentieth-century science. Yet the lie continues to be perpetrated, not on scientific grounds, but because it is what morally justifies our immoral society today. As one teacher of evolution told Ron a few years ago, "I know evolution is scientifically impossible, but I'm still going to teach it because it is morally comfortable." When asked what he meant by that he replied, "As long as I believe I am nothing but an animal, I can live any way I choose. But as soon as I admit there is a Creator, then I become morally responsible to that Creator, and frankly, I don't want to be morally responsible to anyone!"

Evolution begins and ends with a hopelessly illogical premise: Nothing plus chance equals everything! What created the matter and energy necessary to create the universe? The evolutionist has no scientific evidence, so he says, "You must assume by faith that somehow it occurred!"

Spontaneous generation, or the idea that life came from nonliving matter, is postulated as to how life arose. The theory of evolution says that some 3.5 billion years ago there was a large inorganic soup of nitrogen, ammonia,

salts, and carbon dioxide bubbling away. Out of this nox-
ious caldron arose the first single-cell alga. From that came
the rest of the spontaneous steps toward the age of com-
puters.

The problem, of course, is that the evolutionist has no
answer as to where this bubbling, inorganic soup came
from. They always say, "You must assume by faith that
somehow it was there!"

The major problem here is the scientific fallacy of spontaneous generation. Dr. George Wald, Professor Emeritus
of Biology at Harvard University and winner of the Nobel
Prize, wrote in *Scientific American* that spontaneous generation, the idea that life arose from nonliving matter, was
scientifically disproved by Louis Pasteur in 1860. In *Life:
Origin and Evolution* Wald added, "One has only to contem-
plate the magnitude of this task to concede that the spontaneous generation of a living organism is impossible."

Biogenesis is the basic axiom of biology. Biogenesis means
that life only arises from life. It does not come from nonliving matter! The evolutionist's response to this is, "Well,
you must assume by faith that, contrary to the proven laws
of biology, somehow it still occurred!"

The Problem of Reproduction

Another major problem for the evolutionists is Bio-
chemical reproduction. Every cell (no matter how simple)
in plants, animals, and human beings has what is called a
"complex metabolic motor." This is the ability of the cell to
extract energy from its environment in order to supply
energy for the reproduction of the cell and other cell needs.
For life to exist, you must have this metabolic motor. But
this metabolic motor can only be produced by life!

The riddle then becomes: "How, when no life existed,
did substances come into being which are absolutely essential for life, but which can only be produced by life?"

You have the same problem, for example, with DNA,
deoxyribonucleic acid. DNA is the genetic code, formed in
a double-helix strand, which determines the hereditary
characteristics of a human being.

DNA is absolutely essential for life to exist. But DNA can only be produced by life. How, when no life existed, did DNA come into existence? In an interesting sidelight, *Time* magazine published an article a few years ago about a DNA sampling of a cross section of women worldwide. The test covered women of all the major ethnic classifications. The article, titled Mother Eve, showed that the DNA characteristics of all the many women tested went back to one single woman!

The Laws of Probability

Another problem for the evolutionists is the laws of probability, which clearly and simply demonstrate that life from nonliving matter is impossible. As Sir Fred Hoyle, one of the world's leading astronomers and mathematicians, recently said before the British Academy of Science: "The probability of life arising by chance is the same probability as throwing a six on a dice five million consecutive times."

Try that sometime! He then went on to add, "Let's be scientifically honest. We all know that the probability of life arising to greater and greater complexity and organization by chance through evolution is the same probability as having a tornado tear through a junkyard and form out the other end a Boeing 747 jetliner!"

Random impersonal chance does not produce complexity and organization, only greater chaos. Again, the response of the evolutionist to this is, "Well, we must assume by faith that, contrary to the mathematical laws of probability, somehow it occurred!"

Opposing the Second Law

Another major problem is that evolution assumes a gradual upward progression, that things supposedly have evolved from chaos and simplicity to greater and greater complexity and organization—all by chance. The problem is that in this universe we live in, the opposite actually occurs in every single case, according to the laws of physics. All energy and matter are governed by the laws of thermodynamics.

The second law of thermodynamics states that everything in the universe is going from a state of organization and complexity and is running downward, or degenerating toward chaos and disorganization. This is known as the problem of entropy. One only needs to walk through an auto junkyard to see this law in action. No Rolls Royces are rolling out the back gate. The autos rust apart and soon blend with the dust of the ground.

The fact that no one can build a perpetual-motion machine demonstrates entropy. *Everything* loses energy and eventually runs out of energy. Things do not move upward to complexity; instead, things tend to run down. To illustrate further, take that brand-new Rolls Royce like the one we looked for in the junkyard and park it in the woods or mountains and leave it there for five or ten years. What will happen to it? If it is not stolen, the car over time will look like every other car in that junkyard. Like every other physical thing on this earth, it will decay and eventually break down, whether it is a tree or a skyscraper. It will never go upward to greater complexity.

If you have a teenage son or daughter you can test the second law of thermodynamics right in your own home. Just clean their room nice and neat and leave it for a week. You will see entropy at work!

The fact of entropy presents a terrible problem for evolutionists. Some evolutionists have tried to offer solutions like: "We have renewable energy coming from the sun." But random energy never produces organization. In fact, the laws of physics show that it speeds up the process of entropy. Energy does not produce organization or complexity. The energy created at the world's great hydro-electric dams eventually tear up the systems that create our power. Man must continually repair the facilities and the electric systems.

To illustrate, let's say you have a car at the bottom of a mountain. You want to get the car up the mountain. What do you need? You say "energy." So you fill the gas tank with gasoline "energy." Is the car going up the mountain? No. What is wrong? You need a complex mechanism, known as an engine, to transform *random* energy into the *kinetic* energy that is useful for work. But where do you get this complex mechanism? Even if you assume that you have the engine, as the car goes up the mountain it will drive over a cliff. Why? Because it needs a complex system of controls to steer the car. Where does this complex system come from?

Obviously, just having energy does not solve the problem. This is similar to how plants grow. Energy from sunlight is necessary for plants to grow, but the sun's random energy is not enough. Plants must have a complex mechanism, known as photosynthesis, to produce the chlorophyll necessary for the plants' life.

Assuming by Misplaced Faith

The final question we must ask is, How, when no life existed, did these complex mechanisms (such as photosynthesis) which are absolutely essential for life come into existence, since they can only be produced by life? The evolutionist has no logical answer, so again he must say, "You must assume by faith that, contrary to the known laws of physics, somehow it occurred!"

Some evolutionists, such as astronomer Carl Sagan, offer vast time periods as the answer to the dilemma of complexity in nature. They believe that chance plus time will generate increased complexity. So they regularly add more millions or billions of years to their evolutionary hypotheses. But the laws of physics state, "The greater the time span the greater the chaos and disorganization!" Things just do not evolve upward as evolution requires.

To illustrate the above, take an airplane up to 5000 feet and have 100,000 three-by-five cards neatly stacked in it. The theory of evolution would assume that, given enough opportunity, those cards could be dropped out the window and randomly sort and select themselves to spell out "the United States of America" on the ground. You say, "That's ridiculous—they will be flying all over the ground."

Of course it's ridiculous; this is entropy in quick action. Things regress from organization to chaos. So the evolutionist says, "What you need is a greater time span to allow for organization and complexity to take place." But this is like saying that instead of flying at 5000 feet, we'll now take the airplane up to 25,000 feet. Now when we drop those three-by-five cards they will have a greater time span in which to randomly sort and select themselves to spell out "the United States of America" on the ground!

What is going to happen? Remember, it is a basic law of physics that the greater the time span the greater the chaos and disorganization. The cards would be spread over ten times the geography. Every time the evolutionist adds a few more million years to his hypothesis, he is simply hammering another nail into his own coffin!

The Truth About the Fossil Record

Another major problem for evolutionists is the fossil record. Charles Darwin believed that if evolution were true we would find the evidence in the fossil record. He predicted that the geological strata would reveal a gradual upward evolution of species to greater and greater complexity. *Newsweek* magazine of March 29, 1982, had a cover story entitled "Mysteries of Evolution." It contained the following admission:

> . . . a professional embarrassment for paleontologists: their inability to find the fossils of transitional forms between species, the so-called "missing link."
>
> Darwin, and most of those who followed him, believed that the work of evolution was slow, gradual and continuous and that a complete lineage of ancestors, shading imperceptibly one into the next, could in theory be reconstructed for all living animals. In practice, Darwin conceded, the fossil record was much too spotty to demonstrate those gradual changes, though he was confident that they would *eventually* turn up. But a century of digging since then has only made their absence more glaring. Paleontologists have devoted whole careers to looking for examples of gradual transitions over time, and with a few exceptions they have failed.

What we find in the fossil record is all species fully formed with no transitional intermediates or missing links! If evolution were true, we should be finding literally *millions* of transitional forms or "missing links" from one species to the next. Instead we find none! Rather, everything is "after its own kind." As Dr. Duane Gish, who received his Ph.D. in Biochemistry from the University of California at Berkeley, pointed out in *Acts and Facts* (published by the Institute of Creation Research, El Cajon, CA):

> The fossil record shows the sudden appearance, fully formed, of all the complex invertebrates (snails, clams, jellyfish, sponges, worms, sea urchins, brachiopods, and trilobites) without a trace of ancestors.

He goes on to add:

> The fossil record also shows the sudden appearance, fully formed, of every major kind of fish (supposedly the first vertebrates) without a trace of ancestors. This proves beyond a reasonable doubt that evolution has not occurred. If evolution has occurred, our museums should contain thousands of fossils of intermediate forms. However, not a trace of an ancestor or transitional form has ever been found for any of these creatures!

To sum up: we have never observed evolution in the fossil record and we have never observed evolution in the natural world. Evolution is a theory that exists only in the imaginations of evolutionists!

Where Is the Logic?

The question we must ask is: Is it more logical, rational, and scientific to believe in evolution, or is it more logical, rational, and scientific to believe that "In the beginning God created"? Let's look at the evidence.

Does life arise spontaneously by chance, as evolution teaches? No! The basic axiom of all of biology is *biogenesis:*

Life only arises from life; it does not come from nonliving matter. Does this more logically fit evolution or creation?

What about the teaching of evolution that everything is evolving ever upward to greater and greater complexity, all by chance? The evidence is the second law of thermodynamics. The laws of physics show that everything goes from organization downward to chaos. This is known as *entropy*. Does this more logically fit evolution or the biblical account of creation and the fall?

What about the fossil record? Darwin said that if evolution were true we would find the evidence in the fossil record by finding millions of transitional forms or "missing links." What we find, in fact, is everything appearing fully formed after its own kind in the fossil record with no evidence of transitions! Does this more logically fit evolution or biblical creation? In Genesis chapter 1 doesn't God say He created everything "after their own kind"?

It never ceases to amaze us that when we were in kindergarten they taught us that a frog turning into a prince was a nursery fairy tale, but when we got to college they told us that a frog turning into a prince was science! The Bible says that only a fool says in his heart, "There is no God" (Psalm 14:1). By following evolution we have literally become a nation of fools following a false, unscientific idea.

Why Do They Teach It?

Some people have asked us, "If there is no evidence for evolution, why do teachers continue to propagate it in our universities and schools?" Dr. Phillip E. Johnson, Professor of Law at the University of California at Berkeley, has written a book exposing the falsehood of evolution entitled *Darwin on Trial*. He was speaking at a conference when he was asked this question. His reply was very interesting coming from someone within the academic community:

> Most professors continue to teach evolution in the universities out of fear. This fear is that of not being tenured, of not getting research grants, of not being published, and of not being accepted by their peers.

So to be accepted, to be published, to be granted research money, and to be tenured by their university, they must follow the party line, which is evolution. This is how the academic game is played!

Another reason, we believe, why evolution continues to be taught in spite of the contrary evidence is the educational mindset that grips our schools today. Our schools have essentially "ruled out the answer before they asked the question." They have said, "There is no God! Now let's ask the question: What is the Origin of Life?" The reason they never find the answer is because they ruled it out before they asked the question! It is highly unscientific and antiintellectual to rule out answers before you ask questions.

That is no different from going to a math class and having the professor tell you the first day, "There is no number 4. Number 4 does not exist. Number 4 is simply the figment of some fundamentalist imagination." Then you go back to class the second day and the professor asks you the question "What is 2 plus 2?" You answer "3" or "5", but it cannot be 4, because 4 doesn't exist!

The problem is that when you do this you are no longer involved in education but in indoctrination. We have been indoctrinating an entire generation in the false belief that there is no God and that we are simply animals evolved from slimy algae.

The logical end result of this tragedy is a generation of people who don't know who they are, where they came from, or where they are going. We have become a lost generation looking everywhere and trying everything to give us value, self-esteem, and meaning to life.

The Two Sources

Randy Alcorn, founder of Eternal Perspective Ministries in Oregon, summed it all up concisely in a recent article entitled "The Two Sources of Self-Esteem."

Everywhere in the secular media I've been hearing and reading about the critical problem of poor self-esteem among our young people. A bad self-image is being cited as the cause of teen suicide, drug abuse, crime, and violence. Educators and community leaders are trying to find ways to help children bolster their self-esteem.

Where does this plague of low self-esteem come from? Ironically, straight from the atheistic evolutionary view of man with which society has indoctrinated our young people. Where can they get a healthy and accurate self-esteem? From the very Judeo-Christian ethic society is rejecting, and trying so desperately to keep out of the classrooms and public life.

Let me summarize the secular and Christian foundations for self-esteem, then you tell me whether it's any wonder why America's children are feeling like they, their lives, and their values have so little meaning.

The Secular Basis for Self-Esteem

You are the descendant of a tiny cell of primordial protoplasm that washed up on an ocean beach 3½ billion years ago. You are the blind and arbitrary product of time, chance, and natural forces. Your closest living relatives swing from trees and eat crackers at the zoo.

You are a mere grab bag of atomic particles, a conglomeration of genetic substance. You exist on a tiny planet in a minute solar system in an obscure galaxy in a remote and empty corner of a vast, cold, and meaningless universe. You are flying through lifeless space with no purpose, no direction, no control, and no destiny but final destruction.

You are a purely biological entity, different only in degree but not in kind from a microbe, virus, or amoeba. You have no essence beyond your body, and at death you will cease to exist entirely. What little life you do have is confined to a fragile body aimlessly moving through a world plagued by war, famine, and disease. The only question is whether the world will manage to blow itself up before your brief and pointless life ends on its own.

In short, you came from nothing, you are going nowhere, and you will end your brief cosmic journey beneath six feet of dirt, where all that is you will become food for bacteria and rot with worms.

Now . . . why don't you feel good about yourself?

The Christian Basis for Self-Esteem

You are a special creation of a good and all-powerful God. You are the climax of His creation, the magnum opus of the greatest artist in the universe. You are created in His image, with capacities to think, feel, and worship that set you above all other life forms. You differ from the animals not simply in degree but in kind.

Not only is your kind unique, but you are unique among your kind. God has masterminded the exact combination of DNA and chromosomes that constitute your genetic code, making you as different from all others as every snowflake differs from the rest.

Your Creator loved you so much and so intensely desires your companionship and affection that, despite your rebellion, He gave the life of His only Son that you might spend eternity with Him. If you are willing to accept the gift of salvation, you can become a child of God, the King of the universe.

As a Christian, you are clothed with the righteousness of Christ. He has given you special gifts and abilities to serve him in a particular and unique way.

Your heavenly Father is sovereign, and will allow nothing to cross your path that is not Father-filtered. He cares for you so much that He is totally available to you at all times, and listens to every word you say. He cares deeply about your hurts, and has a perfect plan for your life. He has given you the inspired Word of God as a road map for living. He gives you the truth that sets you free, a life that is abundant and eternal, and a spiritual family that loves and needs you.

Your destiny is to live forever in a magnificent kingdom, to reign with Christ over the universe. You will forever enjoy the wonders of His presence and the marvels of His creations. You will spend eternity in intimate and joyful fellowship with your beloved Lord and your precious spiritual family.

Now . . . how does that make you feel about yourself?

Theistic Evolution

One final point that needs to be addressed here is the teaching of "theistic evolution" or the belief that God used evolution to create the world. Sadly, this idea has been widely adopted by many Christian colleges and churches today in the misguided belief that they are able to compromise Scripture to accept evolution.

Some Christian academics, in order to hide their belief in evolution and make it sound more acceptable to their constituency, have renamed this teaching "progressive creationism." They are being not only scientifically dishonest, but biblically dishonest as well.

First of all, "theistic evolution" or "progressive creationism" is a nice idea—if there was any evidence for evolution! The problem is that there is no evidence for evolution, theistically or naturalistically!

Second, why would a perfect God use an imperfect means to create a perfect world? Evolution requires two things: 1) *chance* and 2) *massive death and destruction* through the survival of the fittest.

The theory of theistic evolution teaches that millions of species died out in order to create Adam and Eve. When evolution got to that point after billions of years, then God supposedly started the human race and gave man a soul. But Romans 5:12 tells us there was no death prior to sin, and sin came through one man, Adam. How could you have massive death and destruction over millions of years to get to Adam if there was no death prior to sin?

The main problem for theistic evolutionists seems to be the nature of God, the geology of the earth, the size of the cosmos, and the distance of stars.

First of all, they try to help God out by making the days of creation in Genesis chapter 1 to be long periods of time involving billions of years. This is because they have a very small concept of who God is. If you understand the nature of God you realize that He did not even need six 24-hour days for creation. If you understand the omnipotence of God, He could have done it in six seconds!

Second, theistic evolutionists hold to a uniformitarian view of geology, which is a foundation stone of evolution. This view, created by atheist Charles Lyell in the nineteenth century, states that the earth has changed slowly and gradually through the ages by means of processes that are still going on today. Those who hold to this view, including theistic evolutionists, deny the worldwide flood at the time of Noah as recorded in Genesis chapter 7.

They must reject the universal flood because a cataclysm of this magnitude would destroy their entire uniformitarian view of geology. This is why theistic evolutionists in many Christian colleges and seminaries teach the idea of a local flood located just in the Middle East area. But this is not what the Bible teaches!

Theistic evolutionists have bought into the false idea of the geological column and the dating of the earth by it. The geological column was invented in the nineteenth century by Charles Lyell. He divided the earth into 12 so-called earth ages. These earth ages were based upon the philosophical assumption of evolution that many millions of years were required at each stage for things to have evolved. This is why you always see the supposed evolution of life laid out next to the supposed 12 earth ages.

The dating of the earth's strata is then based on what are called "index fossils." These are fossils that Lyell said should be found in each of his 12 ages of the earth. The fossils in each age were determined based upon Darwin's theory of evolution. In geology you date the rocks by the age of the fossils. In paleontology you date the fossils by the age of the rocks. Let me show you the secret con game of evolution and how it works. Sadly, many Christians have naively fallen for it!

If you look in the *World Book Encyclopedia*, found in every school and library, under the title "Fossils" (vol. 7, page 422 of the 1988 edition), you will find this:

Scientists determine when fossils were formed by finding out the age of the rocks in which they lie.

But if you turn to the title "Paleontology" (vol. 15, page 102 of the 1988 edition), you find this:

Paleontology (study of fossils) is important in the study of geology. The age of rocks may be determined by the fossils in them.

This is circular reasoning! By this means you can date anything any age you want.

Strangely, this "geological column" used as the basis of dating the earth in the theory of evolution has *never been found anywhere in the world!* It is a creation of Charles Lyell's imagination. In fact, he created it because he saw it as a way to destroy belief in God, His creation, and the worldwide flood as recorded for us by God in the book of Genesis.

But even if we did find evidence of the "geological column" it would not be proof of evolution. Rather, it would show everything being buried by a worldwide flood in its logical ecological niche!

The last point that seems to confuse theistic evolutionists is the age of the cosmos, which they date based upon the distance of the stars and the time it takes for light to travel from the most distant stars. Based upon their naturalistic assumptions from the "Big Bang" theory, they generally date the age of the universe at around 15 billion years. They claim that the farthest thing we can see is a quasar, which is 15 billion light-years away. Therefore, they say, light must have been traveling through space 15 billion years for us to now see it.

First of all, it is important to understand that there is no way scientifically you can measure out 15 billion light-years. This date is largely based upon the assumption of evolution and the time it would require for the galaxies, stars, and planets to have formed from a Big Bang in order for life to have begun evolving 3½ billion years ago.

Even if we could take a measuring tape and measure out 15 billion light-years (one light-year is 6 trillion miles or the distance light travels at 186,282 miles per second in one year), it would not bother us because God tells us the purpose of the stars in Psalm 19:1:

> The heavens declare the glory of God; the skies proclaim the work of his hands.

Isaiah 40:12,22,26 says:

> Who has measured the waters in the hollow of his hand, or with the breadth of his hand marked off the heavens? . . . He stretches out the heavens like a canopy, and spreads them out like a tent to live in. . . . Lift your eyes and look to the heavens: Who created all these? He who brings out the starry host one by one, and calls them each by name. Because of his great power and mighty strength, not one of them is missing.

Not only does Genesis 1:1 tell us that God created the heavens, but the above passages show that the heavens are intended to declare the glory of God. If the purpose of the stars is to let us know how great and mighty God is, then it is obvious that the God who created the stars would also have created the light simultaneously coming from the stars, so that we could see them in order to glorify Him!

A Christian astronomer said to Ron, after one of his lectures on creation and a young age for the earth, "I have a problem with your young age. As an astronomer, I believe the universe is 15 billion years old based upon the speed of light and the distance of stars." Ron asked him a simple question: "Who ever told you that distance equals time?" What many theistic evolutionists fail to understand is that distance equals time *only in a naturalistic worldview*. God is eternal. God is not limited by time and space. Time and space are only a function of the natural created order. God is outside of time and space. He, in fact, is the *Creator* of time and space! Thus God did not need a Big Bang and billions of years of cosmic evolution. Rather, God created the stars and starlight instantly at the moment of creation.

As Psalm 19 says, "The heavens declare the glory of God; the skies proclaim the work of his hands."

5

Fast Facts on

Freemasonry and the Masonic Lodge

As we deal with Freemasonry and the Masonic Lodge, we know that this is a subject that comes close to home for many of you. Many of you have loved ones who are in the Masonic Lodge. A lot of men who get involved with Freemasonry do not fully understand what they are getting entangled with.

For a number of years now both of us have pursued an intense study on the subject of Freemasonry. Ed spent 20 years in the Mormon Church, where the temple rituals have been directly lifted from the Masonic Blue Lodge degrees. Other portions of the Scottish rites, such as the ordination of the Holy Melchizedek priesthood, were also in common.

In the book *The God Makers*, Dave Hunt and Ed detailed the parallels and the occult origins of each group. What Ed didn't share was that prior to his conversion to Mormonism he was a member of the Masonic youth group, the DeMolay, and that he has a family history of Masonry that goes back over 175 years.

The more we studied Masonry, the more we realized the depth of its satanic hold over those within its "strong Grip." Within the pages of the hundreds of Masonic books and secret ritual manuals we have gathered and read in our research is a tragic story of godly men who have succumbed to the snare of the enemy. They have brought the darkest side of Baal worship into their homes and congregations.

Fleeing the Lodge

Since we have been speaking on this subject we have seen thousands of Masons who have literally fled the Lodge once they have had that mask of deceit removed. In fact, we have seen whole churches repent.

At one church in Southern California the pastor was a 32nd degree Mason, involved in the craft for 40 years, and his entire elders' board were Masons. When somebody gave them one of Ron's ministry tapes, they formed a committee, as churches do, to study if what he was saying was true. After a year they came back with their report, and the pastor and all the elders resigned from the Masonic Lodge. They issued a statement which their church has now adopted that states that no Mason can hold a leadership position in their church.

Ron was speaking at one of the largest churches in South Texas recently. Before he got up to speak on Sunday morning, some of the elders of the church had noticed his tape on Masonry and came to the pastor's office. They said to him, "Why are we allowing this person to speak?" Ron found out that the Sunday school superintendent was the Worshipful Master of the Lodge in town. The chairman of the church was the Supreme Potentate of the Shrine, and many of the elders were Masons.

When they confronted Ron, he responded, "Everything I share on this tape is documented from your own Masonic authority, as you will hear tonight. If you have a problem with what I say, it's not with me. It's with your own Masonic leaders."

These leaders took the tape back to their Masonic Lodge on Sunday night. They spent till four in the morning going through the documentation from their own Masonic library. On Monday morning they came back and said, "Ron, we want you to know we all resigned from the Lodge last night. We did not realize what we were involved with."

Ed has had similar experiences. In one church in Florida, the Masons in the church threatened the pastor with harm if he allowed Ed to speak. (The church was heavily populated with Masons.) They let the pastor know that Ed was in serious physical danger, and the church office was receiving threatening phone calls. In the Sunday morning service Ed spoke on the subject of Mormonism and promised to speak on Freemasonry that night. Both Ed and the pastor were physically shoved about in the hallway after the service. Things were very tense, but the pastor, a godly man, was determined to deal with Freemasonry that night.

Near the end of the evening service Ed had an altar call for those who wanted to renounce Freemasonry and get right with the Lord in the matter. Many Masons came forward, and many didn't. But Ed will never forget the words of the pastor to his congregation later, at the end of that service.

Speaking directly to the Masons in the congregation, he said, "Dear brothers, I must tell you that I will give you one week to repent and leave Freemasonry or leave this church. If you refuse to do either, we will remove your name from the rolls next Sunday. If you think you can remove me, then have a business meeting and vote me out if you can, for I will not be pastor of a church that has allowed Freemasonry to take root within it."

A large number of his congregation did leave. But something special happened there: A new, freer spirit was present in the church. Worship was deeper and giving increased, surpassing the church income that had come from the Masons. Plus new people came and overflowed the pews in a greater number than ever before.

Most Masons get involved with the Lodge out of peer pressure: Their friends are in it or their grandfather was in it. Some go into it for business reasons: They see it as a way to progress in their business and social lives. Others are attracted by the secret, mystic rituals and symbolism of Freemasonry. Others see people like the Shriners parading around in the red fezzes, riding their funny cars in parades when the Shrine circus comes to town.

How About the Shriners?

People wonder, "Well, what about the Shriners? We hear about the Shriners' Hospital, about Masonic homes for Masons, about all the good works they do. Everyone knows about the Shrine Circus and the many people who are helped by them. Why are you criticizing them? Are you saying that they have something to hide from the world?"

Yes, we are saying just that. This is clearly the case with the Shriners. Their public image is that of a fun-time group pouring out millions of dollars into charity, all the while dressed up in a party spirit, wearing their red fezzes with great aplomb.

The fez itself is an example of the double meaning behind most of Freemasonry's facade. Worn by every Shriner and even carried to the grave with pompous dignity, the history of the fez is both barbaric and anti-Christian. In the early eighth century, Muslim hordes overran the Moroccan city of Fez, shouting, *"There is no god but Allah, and Muhammad is his prophet."* There they butchered the Christian community. These men, women, and children were slain because of their faith in Christ, all in the name of Allah, the same demon god to whom every Shriner must bow in worship, with hands tied behind his back, proclaiming him the god of his fathers in the Shrine initiation, at the Altar of Obligation.

In usual occult fashion, the initiate swears that he will be inseparably obligated to this "most powerful and binding oath" *in advance,* and that he may *never* retract it or depart from it.

The Shriners' blood oath and confession of Allah as God is documented in the secret Lodge document *The Mystic Shrine: An Illustrated Ritual of the Ancient Arabic Order Nobles of the Shrine,* 1975 Edition (pages 20-22). Remember that Allah is *not* just another name for God. Allah is the name of another god.

During the butchering of the people of Fez, the streets literally ran red with the blood of the martyred Christians. The Muslim murderers dipped their caps in the blood of their victims as a testimony to Allah. These bloodstained caps eventually were called *fezzes* and became a badge of honor for those who killed a Christian. The Shriners wear that same red fez today, with the Islamic sword and crescent encrusted with jewels on the front. The greatest tragedy is that the fez is often worn by men who profess to be Christians themselves. It must cause God to weep that *any* Christian man would wear such a blaspemous thing, even in ignorance!

We are going to discover that all those good works are simply an outer shell of an inner darkness. We are going to peel away all the outer wrapping. We will expose very clearly what Freemasonry is, and why no Christian has any business being a part of the Masonic Lodge.

There are over six million Masons worldwide today. There are about 33,700 lodges, the meeting places for the Masons. In the United States we have four million members and 15,300 lodges. Again, most Masons get into Freemasonry for business or social reasons, while others see it as a philanthropic organization of good works, or as a fraternal organization and a brotherhood. Many go into it out of pride, in the belief that through their good works they can save themselves.

The Ritual Journey

The journey into Freemasonry begins at what is known as "The Blue Lodge." The Blue Lodge is the foundation of all Freemasonry. These are the many local lodge groups scattered across the country in almost every little town and city. When a man goes into it he is initiated into The Blue Lodge through three degrees: the first, or "Entered Apprentice Degree," the second, or "Fellowcraft Degree," and the third, or "Master Mason Degree."

After going through the three degrees of The Blue Lodge, the Mason has the choice to stay in The Blue Lodge or to seek the advanced degrees through either the Scottish Rite or the York Rite. Many Masons will go through both.

Within the Scottish Rite there are the fourth through the

thirty-second degrees, plus the thirty-third honorary degree. The York Rite has thirteen degrees. Once the Mason has attained the thirty-second degree, through either higher arm of the craft, he has the option of petitioning to join the Shriners.

Many people think that Masons and Shriners are one and the same, but actually the Shrine is a separate body of the craft. Shriners are Masons who have achieved the highest degrees of The Blue Lodge, and Scottish or York Rites Masonry, who enter into what is known as "The Ancient and Arabic Order of the Nobles of the Mystic Shrine."

Every step of Masonry has its ritual initiation, the mildest being at The Blue Lodge level. Even this is bizarre, to say the least. In order to join the Lodge, each Mason must first be initiated through an initiation ceremony which is similar throughout the world.

The typical ceremony begins with the initiate being first divested of his jacket and his tie and any money or metal articles he has. His left trouser leg is then rolled up over the knee, his shirt is opened to expose his left breast, and his right shoe is removed and replaced by a slipper. Then the person who is to be initiated will have a blindfold put on him and a noose put around his neck. This is called a "Cable Tow." The blindfolded initiate (they call this being "hoodwinked") is brought, with the noose around his neck, to the outer door of the Lodge.

The candidate thus attired is said to be in darkness, an allegory of Masonry that signifies that everyone outside of Masonry is in darkness and that only Masons have the true knowledge that will bring light to the world.

The new Mason is brought to the outer door seeking the light of the Lodge, and there the Doorkeeper, or Tiler, will put a sword or a sharp point to his breast and lead him into the lodge room, where an altar sits in its center. The lodge members await the candidate in the darkness that surrounds the altar, which is lit from a single light above. Behind the altar stands a man called "The Worshipful Master." He is the master of the Lodge and presides over the initiation.

When the initiate is brought before him, he bows before "The Worshipful Master" and says something like this: "I am lost in darkness, and I am seeking the light of Free-masonry." He is then told he is entering into a secret organization and that he must keep the secrets he is going to be taught.

At this time he is required to take a blood initiation oath. Every Mason who joins the Lodge takes his thumb or his hand to his throat and repeats an oath that has been re-peated by every Mason who has joined the Lodge. In the Entered Apprentice or first level of The Blue Lodge, this includes the following words:

> Binding myself under no less a penalty than having my throat cut across, my tongue torn out by its roots, and buried in the rough sands of the sea. . . .

When the new Mason goes into the second degree, or the Fellowcraft Degree of Masonry, the oath includes the fol-lowing words:

> Binding myself under no less a penalty than that of having my left breast torn open, my heart plucked out and given as prey to the wild beasts of the fields and the fowls of the air. . . .

Then, in the third degree, or the Master Mason's Degree, every Mason must swear an oath that includes the follow-ing:

> Binding myself under no less a penalty than that of having my body severed in twain, my bowels taken from thence and burned in ashes. . . .

Masons will tell you that there is nothing wrong in being a Christian and also being a Mason. When they are ex-posed to some of the anti-Christian secrets of Masonry they reply, "Well, those are in the high degrees. We don't know about those things. I'm just in The Blue Lodge." But that is just not true.

The Message of the Bible

The Blue Lodge Mason who also claims to be a follower of Jesus Christ has to ask himself some basic questions. First of all, "How can I put a blindfold on, come before a man I call The Worshipful Master, and say I am lost in darkness and need the light of Freemasonry?"

The Bible brings us a very different message about light and darkness, one that brings with it the hope of joy:

> We write this to make our joy complete. This is the message we have heard from him and declare to you: God is light; in him there is no darkness at all. If we claim to have fellowship with him yet walk in the darkness, we lie and do not live by the truth. But if we walk in the light, as he is in the light, we have fellowship with one another, and the blood of Jesus, his Son, purifies us from all sin (1 John 1:4-7).

How can a Christian Mason say he is lost in darkness and seek to join the Lodge because he needs the light of Freemasonry? The Bible says if you are a Christian and say you are in darkness, you are living a lie, and the truth is not in you. If Christ lives in your life, you have *The Light*.

The second thing the Christian Mason must ask himself is this: "If I am going to join the Lodge, how can I come before a man called "The Worshipful Master" and bow before him in a religious ceremony and say I am lost in darkness?"

Jesus said, "No one can serve two masters. Either he will hate the one and love the other, or he will be devoted to the one and despise the other. You cannot serve both God and Money" (Matthew 6:24).

Jesus said that we cannot serve two masters. We can't claim to be a follower of Christ and then bow before a man we accept as our Worshipful Master any more than we can bow before a Buddha. The money that Christ warned us about fits right into the lodge. What is it if not the prestige, wealth, power, and position among men promised by Lodge membership?

The third thing we must ask is how a Christian can take a pagan blood oath. How can a man who says he is a follower of Jesus Christ swear to have his throat cut from ear to ear and his bowels ripped open and given to the beasts in the field as a penalty for breaking such an ungodly oath?

Most Masons respond by saying that these oaths are just some kind of spooky college-fraternity-type stuff that means little or nothing. But in the fifth chapter of the book of James we are warned:

> Above all, my brothers, do not swear—not by heaven or by earth or by anything else. Let your "Yes" be yes, and your "No," no, or you will be condemned (James 5:12).

God's Word says that the penalty for taking Masonic oaths is *condemnation*. God isn't amused by this. He absolutely forbids taking these pagan blood oaths of Masonry.

But what is it that must be kept so secret? Why is it that Masons are required to take these pagan blood oaths of secrecy not to reveal the secrets of Masonry even before they are told what they are supposed to keep secret? Why must these men bow down while still in ignorance of the secrets to which they are being bound? Why would a man who would never buy a car or a home or enter into a business agreement without first studying all the terms kneel blindfolded in a Lodge room with a noose around his neck and swear obedience to things he has no understanding of?

Roland Blackmore, a Masonic scholar, states, "It is a lamentable fact that the mass of our membership are ignorant of everything connected with Freemasonry." Steinmetz, another Masonic scholar, writes:

> Most of the truly great Masonic writers have deplored the lack of esoteric Masonic knowledge among the Craft in general. The average Mason is lamentably ignorant of the real meaning of the Masonic symbols, and knows as little of its esoteric teachings.

As Masons go through the steps of the Lodge, they experience a series of rituals with symbolism and allegories that represent a very specific religious worldview and philosophy. Many Masons are ignorant of what this is. They become puzzled when asked to define the goal of Freemasonry. Most will say something about *the fatherhood of God and the brotherhood of man*, or about *making good men better*.

The Builders

Perhaps the most widely read and influential book among Masons today is the book written by Joseph Ford Newton entitled *The Builders*. In it he says that the goal of Masonry is "to bring about a universal league of mankind and to form mankind into a great redemptive brotherhood." Newton declares that as Masonry expands, all religious dogmas will cease to be, all individual creeds and doctrines will be done away with, and what remains will be *"The One Eternal Religion"* that Masons are bringing to the world.

Newton goes on to say:

> Why does Masonry seek to change the world? Because Masonry teaches that all non-Masons are living in spiritual darkness. The ritual of Masonry for the first degree, the Entered Apprentice, teaches a candidate that he is long been in darkness and now wishes to be brought to the light of Masonry. The Lodge teaches that only true Masons are enlightened and live in the truth.

The goal of Masonry, according to its leading authorities, is to do away with religions and their creeds and doctrines, and to establish a one-world, universal religion free from the confining dogma of such narrow scope as is found in Christianity. We need to remember that Masonry only requires its members to have a belief in *any god*. The identity is not important.

This is a key element in the puzzle of Freemasonry. The Mason will be zealous in seeking first the lost name of that god or deity and then in accepting the Masonic god as the one, true god over all. When we reveal his name, you will see why it is hidden from the initiates.

Morals and Dogma

Many Masons do not understand this because their own Masonic authorities have been deliberately deceiving them. The most universally accepted authority on Freemasonry is the great Masonic scholar Dr. Albert Pike, who wrote what is termed by many to be the "Bible of Masonry." It is titled *Morals and Dogma of the Ancient and Accepted Rite.*

Albert Pike was the Sovereign Grand Commander of the Southern Supreme Council, A.A., Scottish Rite, for 32 years. He wrote *Morals and Dogma* as the supreme authority of Masonic doctrine. In fact, the current Sovereign Grand Commander, C. Fred Kleinknecht, says, "Pike's great book, *Morals and Dogma*, is the most complete exposition of Masonic philosophy there is."

We will quote from some of Albert Pike's teachings in *Morals and Dogma*, to give you some insight on what is really lurking behind those Lodge doors. Page numbers will be from that book unless otherwise noted.

> The Blue Degrees are but the outer court or portico of the Temple. Part of the symbols are displayed there to the Initiate, but he is intentionally misled by false interpretations. It is not intended that he shall understand them, but it is intended that he shall imagine that he understands them. Their true explication is reserved for the Adepts, the Princes of Masonry. . . . It is well enough for the mass of those called Masons to imagine that all is contained in the Blue Degrees (page 819).

> Masonry, like all the religions, all the mysteries, hermeticism and alchemy, *conceals* its secrets from all except the adepts and sages, or the elect, and uses false explanations and misinterpretations of its symbols to mislead those who deserve only to be misled; to conceal the truth, which it calls light, from them, and

to draw them away from it. Truth is not for those who are unworthy or unable to receive it, or would pervert it (pages 104-105).

Many Masons who go into The Blue Lodge do so out of ignorance, viewing it as a philanthropic organization and never understanding what they are really involved with. The first secret of the Lodge is the fact that Freemasonry is a religion. Most Masons will say that is it not a religion, but simply a brotherhood, a fraternal organization. Yet, as they describe the workings of the Lodge, they are talking religion.

The problem is that Masonry fits every category of what a religion is, according to every definition of religion. In fact, Albert Pike says, "Every Masonic Lodge is a temple of religion, and its teachings are instruction in religion (page 213).

> Masonry is the legitimate successor from the earliest times the custodian and depository of the great philosophical and religious truths, unknown to the world at large, and handed down from age to age, in an unbroken current of tradition, embodied in symbols, emblems, and allegories (page 210).

Pike says that Masonry is:

> the universal, eternal, immutable religion, such as God planted it in the heart of universal humanity. No creed has ever been long-lived that was not built upon this foundation. . . . The ministers of this religion are all Masons. . . . Its sacrifices to God are good works . . . and perpetual efforts to attain to all the moral perfection of which man is capable (page 219).

Masonry is a natural religion without the need of revelation; *everything* in nature is part of God and part of the infinite thought of God. Creation becomes God itself. It is very interesting to note what Paul said about this in the book of Romans.

Although they knew God, they neither glorified him as God nor gave thanks to him, but their thinking became futile and their foolish hearts were darkened. Although they claimed to be wise, they became fools and exchanged the glory of the immortal God for images made to look like mortal man and birds and animals and reptiles. Therefore God gave them over in the sinful desires of their hearts to sexual impurity for the degrading of their bodies with one another. They exchanged the truth of God for a lie, and worshiped and served created things rather than the Creator— who is forever praised. Amen (Romans 1:21-25).

Albert Pike did not say things he didn't mean. His writings are corpulent with evidences of the true nature of Freemasonry.

We belong to no one creed or school. In all religions, there is a basis of truth, in all there is pure morality. . . . All teachers and reformers of mankind we admire and revere. Masonry has her mission to perform. . . . She invites all men of all religions to enlist under her banner (page 311).

It [Masonry] reverences all the great reformers. It sees in Moses, the lawgiver of the Jews, in Confucius and Zoroaster, in Jesus of Nazareth, and in the Arabian iconoclast, great teachers of morality, and eminent reformers, if no more, and allows every brother of the Order to assign to each such higher and even divine character as his creed and truth require. . . . Masonry is a worship, but one in which all civilized men can unite . . . (pages 525, 526).

The first Masonic teacher was Buddha (page 277).

Masonry claims to be the center of the one universal religion. As Newton says in his book *The Builders*, Masons are seeking to promote a universal religion in which all creeds and doctrines would be done away with, where individual faith will cease and people will join together in a universal religion of an ubiquitous brotherhood of good works. Masons say that religion is the experience of relating to God, and that Masonry is the experience of relating to mankind. While separate, they can and do naturally coexist.

Now let us look at a few of the Lodge's basic principles in the light of biblical truth.

No Other Gods

> And God spoke all these words: "I am the Lord your God, who brought you out of Egypt, out of the land of slavery. You shall have no other gods before me. You shall not make for yourself an idol in the form of anything in heaven above or on the earth beneath or in the waters below. You shall not bow down to them or worship them; for I, the Lord your God, am a jealous God, punishing the children for the sin of the fathers to the third and fourth generation of those who hate me" (Exodus 20:1-5).

This is the first and primary commandment. All the other commandments find their reason in it. God put it at the top of the list for a reason: If you have a faulty view of God, your whole spiritual perspective is skewed by that error. Listen to God:

> This is what the Lord says—Israel's King and Redeemer, the Lord Almighty: I am the first and I am the last; apart from me there is no God (Isaiah 44:6).

If your view of God is anything but that which God Himself has declared above, your view is not Christian orthodoxy. If your view of Christ is not that which is biblically based, your view of Christ is filled with danger.

Let us see what the Masonic fraternity has to say about the nature of God.

Bowing at Every Altar

> The true Mason is not creed-bound. He realizes with the divine illumination of his Lodge that as a

Mason his religion must be universal: Christ, Buddha, or Mohammed, the name means little, for he recognizes only the light and not the bearer. He worships at every shrine, bows before every altar, whether in temple, mosque or cathedral, realizing with his truer understanding the oneness of all spiritual truth (*The Lost Keys of Freemasonry*, by Manly P. Hall, 33°, page 65; Macoy Publishing and Masonic Supply Co., Richmond, VA, 1976).

The Bible Says

Jesus answered, "I am the way and the truth and the life. No one comes to the Father except through me" (John 14:6).

There is one God and one mediator between God and men, the man Christ Jesus (1 Timothy 2:5).

Salvation is found in no one else, for there is no other name under heaven given to men by which we must be saved (Acts 4:12).

That is pretty straightforward. The question that has to be asked of the Mason here is simply, "Are you a Christian who confesses that Jesus Christ is Lord?" Is your answer, like that of many Masons, "Yes"?

Then our response to the *Christian* Mason is simply, "Why won't you do what Jesus clearly told you to do?

The Bible Says

You have heard that it was said to the people long ago, "Do not break your oath, but keep the oaths you have made to the Lord." But I tell you, "Do not swear at all: either by heaven, for it is God's throne; or by the earth, for it is his footstool; or by Jerusalem, for it is the city of the Great King. And do not swear by your head, for you cannot make even one hair white or black. Simply let your 'Yes' be 'Yes,' and your 'No,' 'No'; anything beyond this comes from the evil one" (Matthew 5:33-37).

Note that Jesus clearly describes the Masonic oaths and clearly states that these *come from the evil one*—not from fun, not from some kind of macho male bonding, not from some fraternity-type of initiation, *but from the devil.* Jesus Himself said the above quote to those who believed on Him. Surely it would be a foolish man who would defy the Lord in such a serious matter!

Bound by Blood Oaths

From the initiation rituals of The Blue Lodges which we described earlier and through all 33 degrees of Freemasonry, *every Mason in the world is bound by bloody oaths* to maintain the secrets of the Lodge. These binding oaths are kept through the spirit of fear, because the penalties for betraying the brethren of the lodge include serious physical harm to the Mason.

The Bible Says

Jesus, speaking again to His disciples, clearly dealt with this exact situation.

> There is nothing concealed that will not be disclosed, or hidden that will not be made known. What you have said in the dark will be heard in the daylight, and what you have whispered in the ear in the inner rooms will be proclaimed from the roofs. I tell you, my friends, do not be afraid of those who kill the body and after that can do no more. But I will show you whom you should fear: Fear him who, after the killing of the body, has power to throw you into hell. Yes, I tell you, fear him (Luke 12:2-5).

Trusting the Bible

We do well to know the Word of God. As Jesus prayed to the Father for His disciples, His prayer was, "Sanctify them by the truth; your word is truth" (John 17:17). The Bible clearly teaches that the mature Christian must be grounded in God's Word. Ignorance of the Word is probably the most serious shortcoming of those enmeshed in the web of Free-masonry. What true Christian would dare go through the rituals of Freemasonry knowing that someday he or she would have to stand before a holy God and account for those acts of darkness?

The Judgment of the Damned

The Christless end awaiting members of the Masonic order can be demonstrated by the Apron Lecture, given every Mason in The Blue Lodge Ceremony. The following quote can be found almost word-for-word in most Masonic Monitors, the Craft ritual manual.

Each candidate, upon completion of the initiation, is given a white lambskin apron whose pure and spotless surface, he is told, would be—

> an ever-present reminder of purity of life and recti-tude of conduct, and when at last, after a life of faithful service your weary feet shall have come to the end of life's toilsome journey and from your nerveless grasp shall have dropped forever the working tools of life, may the record of your life be as pure and spotless as this fair emblem which I place in your hands tonight, and when your trembling soul shall stand, naked and alone, before the Great White Throne, there to receive judgment for the deeds done while here in the body, may it be your portion to hear from Him who sitteth as the Judge Supreme, the welcome words: Well done, thou good and faithful servant. Thou hast been faith-ful over a few things, I will make thee rule over many things! Enter into the joy of thy Lord.

While the words sound noble, it is actually to the pit of hell that the candidate has been assigned in the subtle words of the message. The promise is that the apron repre-sents the works of the flesh when the Mason stands before God at the Great White Throne judgment.

But there is only one Great White Throne judgment in the Bible, and it is found in Revelation 20:11-15. It is the judgment of *the lost*, who will be judged not by the gift of

God through Christ but by their own works, with an end in the lake of fire. What a tragedy!

The King of the Pit of Hell

In the seventeenth degree of the Scottish Rite, or the Knights of the East and West Degree, after the candidates have completed the initiation they are given the secret password, "Jubulum," and the sacred word, "Abaddon." Here is the clue to the true identity of the Masonic deity. It is revealed in the "sacred word" of this ritual "Abaddon." In Revelation 9:11 we learn that—

> they [the demons and workers from hell] had as king over them the angel of the Abyss, whose name in Hebrew is Abaddon, and in Greek, Apollyon.

Again we must ask, "How could any true Christian dare to take upon himself that evil name as a sacred word?"

The Word Is Out

The supposed quest of The Blue Lodge Masons is the search for "the Lost Word." Most Masonic ritual is concerned with the recovery of this lost word, presumed to be the name of God—supposedly lost through the murder of the architect Hiram Abiff during the building of Solomon's temple. This quest is attained during the ritual of the Royal Arch Degree.

It is here that the secret name of the deity of Masonry is revealed. That name is "Jahbulon."

"Jah" is the short form of the Hebrew name of God, "Yahweh" or "Jehovah." "Bul" is a rendering of the name "Baal." "On" is the term used in the Babylonian mysteries to call upon the deity Osiris. The secret ritual book of the Craft prints the letters J.B.O. It states:

> We three do meet and agree—in peace, love and unity—the Sacred Word to keep—and never to divulge the same—until we three, or three such as we—do meet and agree.

No Royal Arch Mason can pronounce the sacred name by himself. What is represented as the god of Masonry is a three-headed monster so remote from the Christian Trinity and so blasphemous as to damn the soul of anyone who would dare to pronounce its name in a ritual of worship.

Come Out from Among Them

> Do not be yoked together with unbelievers. For what do righteousness and wickedness have in common? Or what fellowship can light have with darkness? What harmony is there between Christ and Belial? What does a believer have in common with an unbeliever? What agreement is there between the temple of God and idols? For we are the temple of the living God. As God has said: "I will live with them and walk among them, and I will be their God, and they will be my people. Therefore come out from them and be separate, says the Lord. Touch no unclean thing, and I will receive you" (2 Corinthians 6:14-17).

One or the Other

Even as Elijah called out on Mount Carmel, "You have abandoned the Lord's commands and have followed the Baals," we cry out, "How long will you waver between two opinions? If the Lord is God, follow him; but if Baal is God, follow him" (1 Kings 18:18,21).

To the Mason reading this chapter, dare you risk laying your Masonic works before the Lord on that last day, covered by an apron of your own works, only to be told, "I never knew you. Away from me, you evildoers!" (Matthew 7:23)?

We pray that you will choose Jesus and be set free from this wicked power unto whom you have submitted your own soul as well as the spiritual headship of your home (and church, if you are a leader in the congregation). Remember this promise:

> If we confess our sins, he is faithful and just and will forgive us our sins and purify us from all unrighteousness (1 John 1:9).

If you are a Mason and are ready to get your life on track with Jesus, pray this prayer right now:

> Father in heaven, in the name of the Lord Jesus I confess that I have sinned. I confess that I have allowed myself to fall under the power and authority of Lucifer, the god of Masonry. I confess it as sin, and ask that You forgive me. I reject it and cast it from me and will immediately remove my name from its rolls. Jesus, I call You Lord and Savior and ask that You come into my heart and fill me with Your love and Holy Spirit. Let no unclean thing remain! I am Yours and Yours alone! I am set free, in Jesus' name. Amen!

6

Hinduism, Yoga, and Reincarnation

By the end of the 1970's Eastern philosophy, based in the religion of Hinduism, was becoming the predominant philosophy in America and Europe. Since Western humanistic philosophy offered no satisfactory answers to people seeking answers to life's questions, the hope was that Eastern philosophy might hold the keys to satisfy man's longing for his meaning and purpose in life.

Hinduism was easily adopted by people as a worldview because it offered many similarities to the Western evolutionary humanism that people had previously tried.

First, it offered a subjective intuitive experience of so-called "reality." But instead of using chemicals like LSD, man could alter his consciousness through Yoga and Hindu forms of meditation, such as the Transcendental Meditation of Maharishi Mahesh Yogi.

Second, Hinduism and Buddhism paralleled evolutionary humanism by offering a continuum of evolution. Man not only had supposedly evolved from slimy algae but could now continue his evolution through transmigration or cycles of rebirth, known in America and Europe as reincarnation.

Third, the Eastern philosophy of Hinduism and Buddhism seemed to give a rationale to many people for the ecology movement. The basic premise of Eastern philosophy is monism. Monism is the Hindu Vedanta philosophy that "all is One." We are One with nature, One with the universe, One with all living things. The cosmos is one intertwined unity with no independent parts. We all share of the same essence or cosmic Oneness.

Thus saving the environment was more than good stewardship; it was an act of saving ourselves. The humanistic desire of man to be God was at first glance compatible with Eastern philosophy in its basic teaching of pantheism. Pantheism means that "all is God" and is the Siamese twin of monism in Hindu teaching. Not only are we supposed to be One with the universe (monism), but the universe *is* God (pantheism). Therefore we are One with God and in fact are God! In Hinduism, though, "God" or "the universe" is by definition "impersonal enlightenment."

The Ultimate Goal

The ultimate goal of Hinduism and Buddhism is to liberate ourselves from this "physical personal existence" and become One with the "Impersonal All." In Hinduism, this "Impersonal All" is often referred to as the Brahman-Atman or the true Reality.

Hinduism and Buddhism teach that people are suffering in life because they have not liberated themselves from their personal world. It is the physical, personal world, they say, that causes suffering. This is because the physical world is really just an illusion, called "maya." In order to get rid of suffering, you must rid yourself of this illusion of physical, personal existence. It is not the true Reality.

"True Reality" is supposedly the Impersonal Brahman-Atman. Therefore you must transcend this physical existence and be absorbed into this "true reality." This is done by transcending this world of illusion by means of Yoga or Transcendental Meditation. You then become part of the Impersonal One, the Brahman-Atman. This is when you achieve "Enlightenment" or Final Liberation. It looks like this:

Hindu Monism (Pantheism)

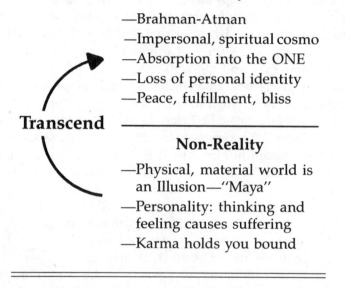

Reality

—Brahman-Atman
—Impersonal, spiritual cosmo
—Absorption into the ONE
—Loss of personal identity
—Peace, fulfillment, bliss

Transcend

Non-Reality

—Physical, material world is
  an Illusion—"Maya"
—Personality: thinking and
  feeling causes suffering
—Karma holds you bound

This state of "Enlightenment" is called by many names. In Hinduism it is called "Moksa," "Samadhi," or "Kaivalya"; in Buddhism it is called "Nirvana"; in Zen it is called "Satori." In the Western countries, terms like "Cosmic Consciousness," "Unified Field of Creative Intelligence," "Absolute Bliss," or "One with Self" are commonly used to refer to this final state.

Yoga: A Spiritual Technique

In Hinduism, Yoga became the main vehicle for transcending this world of illusion. In Sanskrit, the original language of India, "Yoga" means "yoke or union with God" (the Hindu concept of God as the Impersonal All). Yoga, as a religious Hindu teaching and technique, was systematized in India by Patanjali around 200 B.C. In the Western countries, Yoga is commonly thought of as merely the "asanas" or isometric exercises and postures. But to consider it simply as a system of body mechanics is to misinterpret what Yoga stands for and the purpose of its practice.

Yoga is an eight-step process called "Astanga Yoga" (Astanga means "eight steps" in Sanskrit). Its purpose is to help a person achieve transcendence or liberation from this physical, personal existence to the state of Enlightenment. By doing the disciplines of the eight steps, a person can "stop the world and get off!"

This goal is described by the Sanskrit phrase "citta-vritta-mrodha," which means "the stoppage of the mental and physical processes." Radakrishnan, a famous Hindu scholar, says, "The special feature of the Yoga system is its practical discipline, by which the suppression of mental states is brought about through the practice of spiritual exercises."

The first five steps of Yoga are called "Hatha Yoga." These are external, physical disciplines to prepare for the transcendence to the Hindu state of Samadhi or Enlightenment. By discipline of body and mind through isometrics and breathing exercises you seek to detach your mind from the sense organs, until you lose awareness of this physical world, which is said to be an illusion.

At this point a person begins the last three steps of Yoga, called "Raja Yoga." These are the internal meditative techniques for final transcendence. The first step of Raja Yoga is "dharama," or concentration. Patanjali describes it as holding the mind within a center of spiritual consciousness in the body, or fixing it on some divine form (either within the body or outside it). This is often a mantra, which is a word representing a Hindu god.

Then one moves to the second phase of Raja Yoga, which is "dhyana," or meditation. This is continual and unbroken thought directed toward the mantra or object of concentration. At this stage oneness with the universe is achieved, yet with a remaining sense of personal existence.

The final principle of Raja Yoga is "Samadhi," or absorption. At this stage a practitioner achieves unity with the universe without the sense of individual existence.

Hinduism says that this is the stage where you transcend the physical, personal, intellectual, and tactile level of life, and diffuse into the Impersonal Universe. This osmosis is often described in Eastern philosophy as "a drop of water merging into the ocean." The individual eradicates every aspect of his personality to become one with the impersonal monism, "Brahman-Atman."

The problems with Hinduism are seen in its logical conclusions. As A.W. Tozer points out in his classic work *The Knowledge of the Holy:*

> The history of mankind will probably show that no people has ever risen above its religion, and man's spiritual history will positively demonstrate that no religion has ever been greater than its idea of God.

Loss of Personality

If your basic premise of life is Hindu monism and pantheism, that "all is One," "all is God," and "all is impersonal," what does that do to human value and meaning? If the stars are the impersonal God, the clouds are the impersonal God, the trees are the impersonal God, the dirt is the impersonal God, and *you* are the impersonal God, think for a moment: The dirt is God and you are God, so what do you become equal with?

This has historically been the problem in India. Hinduism has never been able to raise the level of nature to the level of humanity. It always ends up in the devaluation of men and women to the lowest level of nature. Not only do we become equal with nature, but we become fully impersonal as well. In Hinduism, not only are we One with the universe, but this universe called God is in reality an empty void which is fully impersonal.

Since the universe is impersonal and we are part of this universe, we too are impersonal. Individual personality is thus destroyed. In Hinduism it is a "drop of water merging into the ocean." Individual identity is lost in the impersonal whole!

Loss of Personal Characteristics

The problem with an impersonal universe is that it destroys personality and all the special characteristics that makes us human. First, the highest expression of human emotions and personality is love and compassion. An impersonal universe never loved or cared about anyone. The meaning of love as a personal commitment of an individual's will is lost. There is no basis for love or human compassion in an impersonal universe!

This is why in Asia, Hindu and Buddhist cultures do not build hospitals or schools; there is no basis for human value. A Hindu swami or Buddhist monk in India or Southeast Asia is known as a "parasite." He does nothing for people. He exists by begging and living off others while renouncing the material world.

Second, there is no basis for morality. As Charles Manson, the cult mass murderer, has said, "If all is One, what is bad?" If "all is One" and "all is impersonal," then there is no difference between good and evil. The "all-encompassing One" contains both good and evil, with no way to distinguish between the two, especially since personality and this physical world are an illusion. Therefore, in Eastern philosophy there can be no difference between us loving you and killing you!

Third, an impersonal universe eliminates human will and freedom of choice. A person's position in life is a result of one's karma in a past life. Karma is the Hindu teaching that actions in one's life will determine a person's fate in the next cycle of life. Thus fatalism dominates countries like India and those in Southeast Asia. Fatalism is the belief that events are fixed in advance for all time in such a way that human beings are powerless to change them. Fatalism destroys any desire for human achievement in life, since everything is already predetermined by fate.

Loss of Science and Technology

In Hinduism, the physical material world is viewed as an illusion. The term for this illusion is "Maya" in Hindu philosophy. As mentioned earlier in this book, science is a body of knowledge and a method of inquiry based on observation and experimentation.

Historically, modern science was developed by people who accepted the empirical evidence that the physical, material world was real. Not only was the world real, but it was created by an intelligent Creator. This basic belief was held by all the founders of modern-day science. This premise led them to the conclusion that their observations and experimentations could be trusted and could achieve logical, intelligent answers.

But if you begin with the Hindu premise that the world is an illusion, how do you observe or experiment with an illusion? It is impossible. This is why science never developed in India; there was no philosophical basis for it. Since there was no basis for science, technology never developed to raise the standard of living in India. It was not until Western philosophy and education, with a basis for science in a Judeo-Christian framework, was introduced through the British in the eighteenth century that India began to develop any form of science and technology.

Today India is turning out many great scientists and engineers. But if you ask them, "Where did you get your education?" you will discover that it was not from Hinduism, but in schools and universities in India founded by Christian missionaries!

Reincarnation

In Eastern philosophy, history or time is viewed as cyclical. Man, according to Hinduism and Buddhism, is caught in an endless cycle of rebirth over and over again, seeking to purge himself of karma and transcend this physical world of illusion.

In India this is known as transmigration. Hinduism teaches that based on the law of karma, your good and bad deeds will determine how you will come back in your next life. If you live a bad life and do not do the things required in Hinduism and Buddhism to renounce this world of illusion, you may come back as a lower form. The possibility of returning as a cow or rat have made both animals sacred in India.

You don't kill a cow in India, since it may be somebody's reincarnated uncle or aunt. That's also why you don't kill the rats. The United Nations now estimates there are over three times more rats in India than the human population. These rats eat nearly one-fourth of the total grain crop!

The idea of transmigration was introduced in 1891 at the World's Fair on Religions in Chicago by a man named Swami Vivikananda. When Vivikananda introduced this idea of transmigration, he discovered that Americans were not very excited about the idea of coming back as a rat, a frog, or a snail. So the concept was changed to reincarnation, which says that you can only come back as another human being. This was much more palatable for Western consumption.

The problem with transmigration or reincarnation is that this cyclical worldview reduces a person to a life determined by impersonal fate. Fatalism becomes the basis of life for the people caught in this system; they will return again and again, thousands of times, until they achieve liberation from this world of illusion.

Their ultimate hope is to transcend to the state of impersonal nothingness. Meaning and purpose to life become nonexistent, except for the quest of denying the reality of this present material world and of merging into the cosmic All. For the Western adherent to the faith, there is always a way out; we can save ourselves through this cyclic rebirth of reincarnation: "Better luck next time."

The Truth About Reincarnation

The first thing that invalidates reincarnation is the fact of the personality of God. Everyone who believes in reincarnation, whether New Agers or adherents of Theosophy, Unity, Hinduism, or Buddhism, all deny a personal Creator. They believe that we are part of an impersonal universe.

The fact that God is personal, that He created us as

personal beings and has personally revealed Himself to us, and that we can have a personal relationship with Him, totally does away with the idea of the need for something like reincarnation.

The second thing that does away with reincarnation is the fact of the atonement of Jesus Christ. The blood sacrifice of Christ on the cross was when He took our sins and nailed them to the cross and covered them with His own blood as the ultimate payment.

Hebrews 10:10 says it was done, once for all time. Christ did for you what you could never do for yourself. Hebrews says He was the eternal lamb of God who shed His blood for your sins and ours. You cannot atone for your sin; only the blood of Jesus Christ can do that.

The third thing that does away with reincarnation is the fact of the resurrection of Jesus Christ. He defeated death and is the living Savior.

Because of this, the fourth reason is the fact of the resurrection of the believer. Jesus said:

> I am the resurrection and the life. He who believes in me will live, even though he dies; and everyone who lives and believes in me will never die (John 11:25,26).

These are two of the most exciting verses in all of Scripture. If you are a Christian, if you have put your faith and trust in Jesus Christ as your personal Lord and Savior, Jesus says you shall never die. When a person takes Jesus Christ as his or her Lord and Savior, He gives them His resurrection power. He has defeated death and is the living Savior. He gives us life eternal.

Second Corinthians 5:8 says that to be absent from the body is to be at home with the Lord. Why? Because Jesus Christ said *He* is the resurrection and the life. If you believe in Him, you shall never die.

Paul says in Philippians 1:21, "To me, to live is Christ and to die is gain." Why is it gain? Because to be absent from the body is to be home with the Lord! That's why Christians are the only ones who can afford to laugh at death. We know where we're going. Death holds no fear for us.

The last thing that does away with reincarnation is Hebrews 9:27, which says that it is appointed unto all of us to die once and that after this comes the judgment—not reincarnation or cyclic rebirth. The worldwide death rate is still one per person. There is coming a day when we will all stand before God. He will ask us one question: "What did you do with the gift of God offered through Jesus Christ?"

7

Fast Facts on

Islam

In this chapter we will examine Islam—what Muslims teach and believe—and how it differs from Christianity. We want to equip you to share the claims of Jesus Christ in a loving and compassionate way with the Muslim. We know that Muslims will be reading these words as well as Christians, and we want to address those readers for just a moment.

If you are Muslim, we want you to know that we appreciate your taking the time to see why your faith is listed in a book about false teaching. There may be some things you will read with which you are in strong disagreement, but we cannot avoid that.

Please understand that in a Western country, where the freedom of religion and freedom of speech are constitutional guarantees, we have the freedom to discuss, consider, and think about religious issues. We have the freedom to say what we want and write what we want. That freedom to think and act for ourselves is vitally important, and is a major difference between our culture and faith and that of Islam.

Ron Carlson knows what he is talking about in this matter. He shares not only from his academic studies (simply from books or theory), but from very practical life experiences as well. Ron studied and lived in the Middle East. He studied Middle Eastern history, archaeology, and Arabic beliefs. He lived and worked in Beirut, Lebanon, and in Palestine, and traveled through many more Muslim countries, such as Morocco, Algeria, Syria, Jordan, Tunisia, Libya, and Egypt.

As a Christian, Ron has spoken in probably every high school (as well as the American University) in Beirut, Lebanon. He has lectured in the Muslim countries of Malaysia, Indonesia, Pakistan, and Bangladesh.

We have both traveled and lectured throughout the Philippines, where the Muslim faith is visible everywhere. Both of us have dialogued the points of this subject with Muslim religious leaders. We share not simply from theoretical book knowledge but from a very live working knowledge of what Islam is in its practical and real sense.

Where the Muslims Are

Islam is a rapidly growing religion, both spiritually and geographically. Today there are approximately 850 million Muslims worldwide. They make up about one-sixth of the world's population. By the year 2000 there will probably be a billion Muslims in the world. Islam now dominates 52 countries of the world.

When most people think about Muslims, they immediately think of the Middle East or North Africa, but in fact only 20 percent of the world's Muslims live in those two areas; most of them live in other countries. The largest Muslim country is Indonesia, with 154 million Muslims. The total Arab world, including all of the Middle East and North Africa, has about 144 million Muslims. Bangladesh has 90 million and Pakistan another 90 million. India has about 70 million Muslims, approximately 11 percent of its population.

To the surprise of many people, there is also a large Muslim population in China. In fact, nearly 63 million Muslims live in China. The whole southern tier of the former Soviet Union along the border with Afghanistan, Iran, Syria, and Iraq (and all across to Turkey), is home for more than 41 million Muslims. In Turkey there are about 46 million and in Iran about 40 million.

Islam is now the second-largest religion in Europe. In Great Britain there are over 1½ million Muslims, with some

1500 mosques. Thirty years ago in the United States Islam was virtually nonexistent. But because of heavy immigration from Muslim countries, with many Muslims fleeing the oppression of the Islamic states and seeking freedom in the United States, there is now a Muslim population of about 5 million in our country.

God gave us a Great Commission: to go into all the world and proclaim the good news of Jesus Christ. But, sad to say, we have not carried that Great Commission as we should have into the Muslim world. Only 2 percent of North American missionaries have been involved in Muslim ministries. We have one Christian missionary for every million Muslims! In the twenty-first century Islam will represent the single greatest challenge to Christianity. No matter how peaceful many Muslims are, their core doctrine allows for no other faith to exist peacefully alongside them.

Understanding Islam

To understand Islam, perhaps the key factor is to realize that Islam must be studied in the religious and cultural context of seventh-century Arabia.

In his excellent book *Islamic Invasion* (Harvest House Publishers), Dr. Robert Morey says that what Muhammad did was to raise the seventh-century culture in which he was born to the status of divine law. In fact, Islam is the deification of seventh-century Arabian culture. Unless you understand the historical context of when and where Muhammad was born, you will never understand Islam.

Dr. Arthur Arberry, the head of Mideastern Studies at Cambridge University (and one of the great Arabic scholars), said this:

> Islam is a peculiarly Arabian religion because Islam is a religion *and* culture, and as a religion and culture they are one. It must be understood in terms of its essential identification with seventh-century culture.

Islam imposes its seventh-century Arabian culture in its political expression, in its family affairs, in its dietary laws, in its clothing, in its religious rites, and in its language. Muslims are religiously compelled to impose seventh-century Arab culture on the rest of the cultures in the world.

Muhammad took the political laws which governed seventh-century Arabian tribes and literally made them the laws of Allah, their God. In such tribes, the sheik or chief of the nomadic tribes had absolute authority. There was no concept of civil or personal rights in seventh-century Arabia. This is why Islamic countries are inevitably ruled by dictators or strong men who rule as despots. There are 21 Arab nations today, and not one of them is a democracy. Democracy cannot flourish in Islam.

The more Islamic fundamentalism gains dominance, the more a nation is plunged back into the dark ages of seventh-century Arabia. Iran is a good example of this. The despots today of Libya, Iran, Iraq, Syria, the Sudan, and Yemen are merely examples of such Arabian tyranny grafted into modern times.

Because there was no concept of personal freedom or civil rights in the tribal life of seventh-century Arabia, Islamic law today does not recognize freedom of speech, freedom of religion, freedom of assembly, or freedom of the press. This is why non-Muslims (such as Christians) are routinely denied the most basic of human rights and are often physically attacked or jailed.

Islam in Action

According to a *Washington Post* story on January 3, 1993, crowds of Muslims, reacting to what they regarded as proselytizing by Christians, attacked or burned several Christian churches or homes on the islands of Java and Sumatra. In the biggest reported incident, more than 10,000 Muslims, apparently well-organized, tore down and burned the home of a Christian preacher outside Perusia, a town in East Java, to protest tracts that he was distributing.

The mob then wrecked two nearby Protestant churches that were unconnected to the preacher. The head of Indonesia's largest Islamic organization says that at least

30 attacks on churches or other Christian property were reported in the previous three months.

The Associated Press reported this on February 8, 1993:

> Western human rights groups say that a quick mobilization by their international networks may have saved the lives of two Christian Philippine leaders imprisoned in Saudi Arabia.
>
> Reliable sources within the human rights community reported that two lay pastors scheduled to be executed on Christmas Day by the government of Saudi Arabia were arrested in October and charged with violating kingdom law by preaching Christianity. The two had apparently been in hiding since January, when a Christian service they led in a private home was raided by Saudi religious police. Reports of the scheduled execution prompted a flurry of international inquiries and protests, including a harshly worded appeal to King Faud from Philippine president Fidel Ramos.

These efforts were futile. The two pastors were beheaded in Saudi Arabia because they dared to hold a Christian Bible study! And this is the same country where Christians by the tens of thousands had just stood in defense of its soil against attacks from Iraq!

There is no freedom of religion in Saudi Arabia. In fact, one of the biggest tragedies of the Gulf War was that when we sent our men over there to save that country of Saudi Arabia, our Christian chaplains weren't even allowed to wear their little crosses on their lapels. The government of Saudi Arabia said they were not allowed to hold Christian chapel services for our soldiers who were protecting their country. Service personnel were advised to leave their Bibles at home. This was because Islamic law forbids any presence or mention of Christianity.

The *Washington Post* of January 13, 1993, carried this story:

> Sudan's radical Islam regime is not just waging a genocidal war in the South against Christians, it is also

part of a larger Islamic push. It made itself a training ground for Islamic terrorists to overthrow Egypt's pro-Western regime. For months now, Islamic terrorists have been going around and randomly shooting foreign tourists in an attempt to kill the major foreign currency earner of a desperately poor country so that they might be turned back to the Islamic laws.

Islamic Practice

Other cultural things that Muhammad took from the culture around him include praying five times a day while facing Mecca in Saudi Arabia. This reminds the Muslim five times a day that he must bow in obedience to Arabia.

A Muslim is also required, often in the face of great hardship and great cost, to go on a pilgrimage to Arabia at least once in his life to worship at the Kaaba in Mecca. Historical evidence is clear in showing that Muhammad adopted the pagan religious rite of a pilgrimage to Mecca, which was already being widely practiced long before Muhammad was even born.

Muhammad, in order to appease the merchants of Mecca (who made tremendous amounts of money by people coming there on pilgrimages), put this requirement into Islam as part of his religion. For financial and cultural reasons Islam adopted this pagan practice, which must be fulfilled even by the poorest Muslims as one of their five pillars of faith.

One of the most demeaning practices of Islam is its barbaric treatment of women. Women are considered property in the fundamental sects of Islam. They are not allowed to have ownership of any kind of property. Approximately 75 percent of Muslim women suffer female circumcision in a most barbaric, painful ritual designed to make them obedient and docile. They are dressed from head to toe in clothes that cover all but the eyes, and often even these are covered by a veil.

It is interesting that what an illiterate nomadic tribesman wore in the desert in seventh-century Arabia is still mandated as the dress code for Muslim women today! It is a clear denial of civil rights to women and is reflective of the Islamic Arabian culture and its low view of women.

You might remember what took place during the Gulf War. On March 10, 1991, *The New York Times Magazine* reported the following incident about women's rights in Saudi Arabia.

The crisis in the Gulf spawned a much-publicized demonstration by women who dumped their chauffeurs and drove in convoy, defying a ban on women driving in Saudi Arabia. The incident prompted a vicious campaign against them by religious fanatics with government acquiescence. The religious police patrolled the streets and shopping malls, telling the women to cover their faces and the young men to pray.

The government punished the demonstrating women as severely as it would any public protester. The women as well as their husbands were forbidden to leave the kingdom. They were forbidden to speak with foreign reporters or to discuss their situation with an outsider. They were warned of further reprisals if they attempted to drive again and stage another demonstration.

But the government's treatment of these women was mild compared to their treatment by the Islamic religious establishment. The fundamentalist sheiks denounced them from one of the kingdom's most powerful political platforms, the Mosque Opus.

In the Friday services after the demonstration, the women were branded as "red Communists, dirty American secularists, whores and prostitutes, fallen women and advocators of vice." Their names, occupations, addresses, and phone numbers were distributed in leaflets at the mosques and other public places. One leaflet accused them of having denounced Islam, an offense punishable by death in Saudi Arabia. And these women were all educated Ph.D.'s, most of them teachers at the University. Some were medical doctors. Yet they were threatened with death because they had gotten into cars and driven them. Several of the women remained unrepentant, convinced that eventually the issue of their status will be addressed.

Islamic Backgrounds

The culture of Muhammad's world was very animistic. Every Arab tribe had its sacred magic stones which they believed protected the tribe. Muhammad's particular tribe had adopted a black stone and had set it in the Kaaba. This magical black stone was kissed when people came on their pilgrimages and worshiped at the Kaaba. It was probably an asteroid or a meteorite which they viewed as being divine. All the nomadic tribes had one of their tribal deities resident in the Kaaba.

The dominant religion just prior to Muhammad was Sabianism, a religion in which heavenly bodies were worshiped. The moon was viewed as a male deity, and a lunar calendar was used. The pagan rite of fasting began with the appearance of the crescent moon. Fasting was later adopted as one of the five pillars of faith of Islam. Fasting in Ramadan, in the ninth month, already preexisted in the Arab culture before Muhammad was even born.

What about the name "Allah"? Muslims claim that Allah is the same God as Christians worship, just under another name. Yet if you look at the history of it, it is very different. The term "Allah" is a purely Arabic term used in reference to an Arabian deity. In fact, Allah was known to pre-Islamic Arabs. He was one of the many deities that already existed in Mecca. The tribe into which Muhammad was born was particularly devoted to Allah, which was the moon god. It was represented by a black stone which was believed to have come down from heaven.

In Arabia the sun god was viewed as female, and the moon was viewed as the male god. In pre-Islamic times, Allah, the moon god, was married to the sun god, and together they produced three goddesses called The Daughters of Allah. They were viewed as being at the top of the pantheon of Arabian deities, those 360 idols in the Kaaba, at Mecca. When Muhammad took control of Mecca, he destroyed all the idols in the Kaaba except the stone deity, Allah. Do not ever accept Allah as just another name of the true and living God!

The symbol of the worship of the moon god, Allah, in pre-Islamic Arab culture throughout the Middle East was the crescent moon. Today the crescent moon is on every flag of an Islamic nation. Go to a mosque; what is on top of it? A crescent moon, the symbol of Allah. Yet many Muslims don't even know why it's there.

Background of Muhammad

Muhammad, the prophet of Islam, was born in 570 A.D. and lived for 62 years, dying in 632. At the time he was born, Mecca was the center of trade and religious activity. Muhammad was a camel driver until the age of 25, when he met and married a lady who was 15 years his senior. She was 40 years old and wealthy.

For the next 15 years, Muhammad ran the family fruit business in Mecca. It wasn't until he was 40 years old that he claimed to receive revelations. He would go, as the seekers of truth would, up to a cave which was about three miles north of Mecca, to pray and meditate.

According to Muslim tradition, the angel Gabriel came to Muhammad. Actually there are four different statements of what happened (in the Koran) which contradict each other. The Muslims have chosen to say now that it was Gabriel, and they take this as a sign that Muhammad was a prophet to the Arabs.

After meditating there off and on for two years, Muslims say, Muhammad received revelations during which he would go into epileptic fits. (That is what Muslims believe they were.) He would shake, he would perspire, he would foam at the mouth. Whether they were epileptic or even demonic, he claimed he then received revelations from an angel of light.

What were the revelations? They were written down into what is known as the Koran, the Islamic holy book. However, they were not written down until years later because Muhammad himself was uneducated and probably did not even know how to write.

The main message that Muhammad was communicating

was that there was no god but Allah, that he was the one true god who created everything. The second thing he taught was that man is God's slave, and it is his first duty to submit to God and to obey him. That's why you get the term "Islam." Islam means, in Arabic, *submission*, and a Muslim is one who submits to the will of Allah. Muhammad said that the chief duty of man is to submit to the will of Allah.

Muhammad also said that a great and terrible day of judgment is coming in which God will raise up the dead to life and will judge them and reward them based upon their deeds. Those who are found worthy will be given a sensuous life in heaven, and those who do not make it will be condemned to hell.

The people at Mecca did not think too highly of this new prophet and his revelations. In fact they began to criticize and attack him. In 622 A.D. he fled to Medina, about 280 miles north of Mecca. This was the beginning of Islam.

In the Middle East, everything is based upon the time that Muhammad fled to Medina in 622 A.D. That is the beginning of the Islamic calendar.

It was in Medina that Muhammad first tried to get the Christians and Jews who were living there to follow him as "the prophet." He called himself a prophet and an apostle, although that term was not used in their culture. He used the term "prophet" to appeal to the Jews and "apostle" to appeal to the Christians.

He told them, interestingly, to pray to Jerusalem. When they did not accept Muhammad as a prophet or an apostle, he rejected them and told the other people to pray to Mecca, to Allah, his tribal deity. He then began to receive more revelations. It is very interesting to note what these revelations were. (They are found in the Koran.) He received revelations that he was to loot and steal from caravans that were passing through. There were many cases in which Muhammad and his followers would loot and rob caravans and then kill the men in order to satisfy his greed. In fact, the Koran and history report that he fought over 66 battles, killing tens of thousands of people.

In one of his revelations, Muhammad was told to kill and drive out all the Jews. One time he had 1,000 Jewish men brought together and had them all beheaded. Islam became known as the religion of the sword. In 628 A.D., Muhammad received a revelation that Islam was to be exalted above all other religions, including Christianity and Judaism.

In 629 Muhammad raised up an army of 10,000 men. He returned to Mecca, where he had been raised, and conquered it. By force, he imposed Islam on the rest of the Arabian tribes. Muhammad died in 632 A.D., having conquered much of the Arabian Peninsula. Islam then spread by the sword across North Africa, and today holds one-sixth of the world's population.

Islam on the Move

Once while Ed was speaking at Utah State University he made the statement that Mormonism is "the American Islam." He drew a comparison between the claims of Muhammad and Joseph Smith, the Koran and the Book of Mormon.

During the question-and-answer time he faced a number of very agitated Muslims. In fact, the Muslim interaction all but overshadowed the dialogue on Mormonism. The next day, Ed met with two Muslim leaders and began a series of contacts that forced him to take a deep look at Islam's history, its tenets of belief, and its comparisons to orthodox Christianity.

Today the 5 million Muslims in the United States add up to more than all the Mormons, Jehovah's Witnesses, and Christian Scientists combined. An extremely militant proselytizing program is under way in many major cities and in every state university we have visited. The Muslims are going to make the Mormon missionary effort look pale by comparison. As orthodox Christians, we are going to have to be ready to deal with what may be the most aggressive attack on Christianity in its history.

The Koran tells us that Muhammad drove the other idols away; his god was now the only god and he was its messenger. But he kept the Kaaba as a holy, sacred place. He obligated every believer to make a pilgrimage to the stone at least once in his lifetime (Sura 22:26-37).

Many people believe that Islam, Judaism, and Christianity are all just kissing cousins. In fact, many Christians teach that Allah is just another name for the biblical God whom we worship. Let's review the basic tenets of Islam and judge it for ourselves.

The Six Beliefs of Islam

1. **God:** There is one true God, named Allah.

2. **Angels:** They are the servants of God, through whom He reveals His will. The greatest angel is Gabriel, who appeared to Muhammad. Everyone has two "recording angels": one to record his good deeds, the other to record his bad deeds.

3. **The Prophets:** Allah has spoken through many prophets, but the final and greatest of these is Muhammad. Other prophets include Noah, Abraham, Moses, and Jesus.

4. **The Holy Books:** The Koran or Quran is the holiest book of Islam, believed to be Allah's final revelation to man. It supersedes all previous revelations, including the Bible. It contains Allah's word as passed on orally to Muhammad by Gabriel. It contains 114 chapters or Suras. Muslims also recognize the Law of Moses, the Psalms, and the Gospels but consider them to be badly corrupted.

5. **The Day of Judgment:** A terrible day on which each person's good and bad deeds will be balanced to determine his fate.

6. **The Decree of God:** Allah ordains the fate of all. Muslims are fatalistic. "If Allah wills it" is the comment of a devout Muslim on almost every situation or decision he faces.

The Five Pillars of Islam

1. **Affirmation** (Shahada): "There is no God but Allah, and Muhammad is his messenger." This is recited constantly by devout Muslims.

2. **Prayer** (As-Salah): Muslims are required to pray five times a day, kneeling and facing Mecca.

3. **Almsgiving** (Zakah): A worthy Muslim must give 2.5 percent of his income to the poor.

4. **The Fast** (Siyam): Faithful Muslims fast from dawn to dusk every day during the ninth month of the Islamic lunar calendar, Ramadan, which is sacred.

5. **The Pilgrimage** (Al-Hajj): Muslims are expected to journey to Mecca at least once in their lifetime.

Some have added a sixth Pillar of Faith to this list, known as **The Holy War** (Jihad). In the early years of Islam, and even often today, the intent is the spread of Islam by force. Islam regards itself as the universal religion. Jihad is viewed as service in the spread and defense of Islam. Today many Muslims who are schooled in Western values take Jihad figuratively to mean the spread of Islam through evangelism.

A Different Gospel

Islam teaches that God is so far above man in every way that He is virtually unknowable. He will send individuals to Paradise or Hell as he chooses.

Islam teaches that Jesus was a messenger of God, not the Son of God. Muslims deny that He is Almighty God come in the flesh. But the Bible says:

> In the beginning was the Word, and the Word was with God, and the Word was God. He was with God in the beginning. Through him all things were made; without him nothing was made that has been made. In him was life, and that life was the light of men.

The Word became flesh and made his dwelling among us. We have seen his glory, the glory of the One and Only, who came from the Father, full of grace and truth (John 1:1-4,14).

Dear friends, do not believe every spirit, but test the spirits to see whether they are from God, because many false prophets have gone out into the world. This is how you can recognize the Spirit of God: Every spirit that acknowledges that Jesus Christ has come in the flesh is from God, but every spirit that does not acknowledge Jesus is not from God. This is the spirit of the antichrist, which you have heard is coming and even now is already in the world (1 John 4:1-3).

Muslims deny that Jesus is divine. The Bible says:

In Christ all the fullness of the Deity lives in bodily form (Colossians 2:9).

Muslims deny that Jesus died on the cross for our sins. (Most believe that Judas died in his place.) They deny that He rose from the dead. The Bible says:

This is my blood of the covenant, which is poured out for many for the forgiveness of sins (Matthew 26:28).

Many of the Jews read this sign, for the place where Jesus was crucified was near the city, and the sign was written in Aramaic, Latin and Greek (John 19:20).

Muslims deny that Jesus is the final, conclusive revelation of God. The Bible says:

In the past God spoke to our forefathers through the prophets at many times and in various ways, but in these last days he has spoken to us by his Son, whom he appointed heir of all things, and through whom he made the universe. The Son is the radiance of God's glory and the exact representation of his being, sustaining all things by his powerful word. After he had provided purification for sins, he sat down at the right hand of the Majesty in heaven (Hebrews 1:1-3).

Is **Allah,** this stone idol, the God of Abraham, Isaac, and Jacob? Just because Muhammad said so doesn't make it so! **Allah** chose Hagar and her son Ishmael for his covenant. **The God of the Bible** chose Abraham's other son, Isaac, as heir to *His* covenant.

> Abraham said to God, "If only Ishmael might live under your blessing!" Then God said, "Yes, but your wife Sarah will bear you a son, and you will call him Isaac. I will establish my covenant with him as an everlasting covenant for his descendants after him. And as for Ishmael, I have heard you: I will surely bless him; I will make him fruitful and will greatly increase his numbers. He will be the father of twelve rulers, and I will make him into a great nation. But my covenant I will establish with Isaac, whom Sarah will bear to you by this time next year." When he had finished speaking with Abraham, God went up from him (Genesis 17:18-22).

Allah is an unknowable being, impossible to approach or comprehend. The chief lack in the Islamic doctrine of God is that of love. The orthodox Muslim cannot say that God is love. **The Bible's God** befriends people like Abraham (Isaiah 41:8) and talks with them (Genesis 18:22ff.). He loved us so much He sent His only begotten Son to die for us!

> For God so loved the world that he gave his one and only Son, that whoever believes in him shall not perish but have eternal life (John 3:16).

> Dear friends, let us love one another, for love comes from God. Everyone who loves has been born of God and knows God. Whoever does not love does not know God, because God is love. This is how God showed his love among us: He sent his one and only Son into the world that we might live through him. This is love: not that we loved God, but that he loved

us and sent his Son as an atoning sacrifice for our sins
(1 John 4:7-10).

Allah is a god you cannot know personally. You know
only the laws and commands of God given through the
prophets, which you must obey and submit to. When a
Muslim prays, he will always pray for mercy because he
does not know the grace of God. He does not know that
God loves us and has provided a Savior for our sins.

The Bible's God delights to show His boundless mercy.
His gospel is the "good news" of grace and forgiveness.
Titus 3:4-7 says:

> When the kindness and love of God our Savior
> appeared, he saved us, not because of righteous things
> we had done, but because of his mercy. He saved us
> through the washing of rebirth and renewal by the
> Holy Spirit, whom he poured out on us generously
> through Jesus Christ our Savior, so that, having been
> justified by his grace, we might become heirs having
> the hope of eternal life.

Allah requires total obedience to Islam and weighs the
works of people. Allah and the Koran relegate Jesus to just
the last prophet before Muhammad, below his authority.
Jesus was not the Way, and could only point the way to
Muhammad.

The Bible's God can only be reached through Jesus
Christ, and trusting Him is the only way to heaven. Jesus
said:

> I am the way and the truth and the life. No one
> comes to the Father except through me (John 14:6).

Allah required the works of Muhammad to complete his
words of judgment *to* man. **The God of the Bible** sent His
son to accomplish the finished work of grace *for* man.

> When he had received the drink, Jesus said, "It is
> finished." With that, he bowed his head and gave up
> his spirit (John 19:30).

In the light of Allah's actual origin and his radical difference from the God of the Bible, we must conclude that Allah is not God. Nor is the name "Allah" a generic Mideast name for God, as many Christians think. *Allah is the name of a false god who cannot save anyone from anything!*

8

Fast Facts on

Jehovah's Witnesses: The Watchtower Bible and Tract Society

In this chapter we want to deal with the very important subject of the Watchtower Bible and Tract Society, headquartered in Brooklyn, New York. This group is more commonly referred to as the Jehovah's Witnesses.

Most of you are probably familiar with the Watchtower through the two major magazines that appear in many public places and also come to us by way of door-to-door visitors.

The Watchtower Organization is best known by its mass publications. In fact, it is the largest publisher in the Free World! In one recent year it printed over 44 million books and over 550 million magazines. Over 14 million copies of the *Watchtower* magazine are published every two weeks in 108 languages of the world. The organization also publishes over 12 million copies of *Awake* magazine in about 62 languages every two weeks.

The Jehovah's Witnesses have mapped out the entire United States so that every residence will be contacted at least once or twice a year by a team of door-to-door workers. They claimed recently that in one year over 3.6 million members spent over 835 million hours of door-to-door witnessing for the Watchtower! Out of that sheer grueling persistence they have been able to harvest many people who have not been grounded in God's Word and were easily led astray by this counterfeit religion.

Beginnings Under Russell

The Watchtower Society was begun by a man named Charles T. Russell, the founding father of the Jehovah's Witnesses. He was raised in a protestant church in Pennsylvania. As he grew up, Russell said there were certain things which he did not like in the Bible. He said he did not like the teaching of hell and eternal judgment or the teaching of the trinity. He said the trinity wasn't rational and he could not understand it.

Russell began to develop his own theology, which he began to publish in a series of volumes called *Studies in Scripture*. Later, in 1879, he began to publish the *Watchtower* magazine. In 1884 he incorporated the organization in Pennsylvania as the Watchtower Bible and Tract Society. In 1909 Russell moved its headquarters to Brooklyn, New York, where it has remained to this day.

Russell is the founding father of the theological errors of the Watchtower. Early in his ministry he calculated when Jesus Christ was going to return visibly to this earth, and for many years he prophesied that Christ would return in 1874.

When Christ did not show up, Russell changed his calculations. For many more years he prophesied Christ's return in the year 1914. But 1914 came and went, and again Jesus Christ failed to show up.

Russell was not disheartened. He redefined the second coming of Christ to mean that Jesus Christ had returned invisibly as an invisible spirit, a ghost, in 1914 to help set up his organization.

Growth Under Rutherford

Russell died in 1916 having been proven a false prophet. The Watchtower Organization was taken over in 1917 by a

very dynamic leader, a man named Joseph Franklin Rutherford. It was under Rutherford's leadership that the Watchtower was built into the great theocratic giant that we know
today.

If you have ever talked at length with a member of the
Watchtower Society, you know that he or she claims it to be
the theocratic kingdom of God on earth. What is meant by
that is a government ruled by God. Jehovah's Witnesses
believe that they are God's government on earth and that
all other governments are satanic. This is why Jehovah's
Witnesses will never salute the flag, why they will never
recite the Pledge of Allegiance, and why they will never
serve in the armed forces of any nation. They believe that
all governments are satanic except the true government of
God, headquartered in Brooklyn, New York.

Jehovah's Witnesses also isolate themselves in other
ways from their neighbors. They don't celebrate Christmas
because they deny the incarnation of Jesus Christ. And
they don't celebrate Easter because they deny the bodily
resurrection of Jesus Christ.

It was under Rutherford's leadership that the name
"Jehovah's Witnesses" began to be used. He said they
would do this to vindicate the true name of Jehovah, since
he claimed that Jesus Christ is not God and the Holy Spirit
is not God, but Jehovah alone is God.

We have no problem with the term "Jehovah." It is
simply an Old Testament identification for God. Actually,
the Jews never pronounce the name of God. When writing
in Hebrew the ancient Jews did not use vowels, only conso-
nants. They spelled this name YHWH, the unutterable
name of God. Most likely it would have been pronounced
"Yahweh," but it has been Anglicized as Jehovah, simply
referring to the Old Testament identification for God.

Rutherford was also famous for his many prophecies. In
fact, he prophesied that the patriarchs Abraham, Isaac, and
Jacob would return visibly to this earth to help promote the
kingdom of God. He was so sure of this prediction that he
built a large palatial mansion in San Diego, California, for

Abraham, Isaac, and Jacob to live in when they would return sometime between 1925 and 1929.

But 1929 came and went and Abraham, Isaac, and Jacob never showed up. That's when Rutherford moved into the mansion himself and lived there until he died in 1942, also proven a false prophet.

Outreach Under Knorr

The organization was taken over in 1942 by a man named Nathan H. Knorr. It was under Knorr's leadership that it developed its strong missionary outreach all over the world. It was also under his leadership that the Witnesses did their own translation of the Bible, which they call *The New World Translation.*

The Jehovah's Witnesses claim that five Greek scholars in the Watchtower did this translation. But it becomes quite obvious to anyone who knows Greek or Hebrew that there are gross errors in this translation. It was obviously produced as a conscious attempt to make the Bible fit preconceived Witness theology.

The new translation was just part of the problems created by Nathan H. Knorr. You would think he had learned a lesson about false prophets from his predecessors. And in fact the man did withstand the urge for many years. But finally, in 1966, he could no longer resist, and Knorr also began to prophesy through the *Watchtower* and *Awake* magazines. His first major prophecy was that the year 1975 was going to be the end of the age and that Armageddon would occur at that time. Obviously 1975 has come and gone and Armageddon did not occur. It was just too big a lie to weave a new tale around.

Many Jehovah's Witnesses understood what God had said in Deuteronomy 18:20-22, where He gave us the biblical test for a prophet.

> A prophet who presumes to speak in my name anything I have not commanded him to say, or a prophet who speaks in the name of other gods, must be put to death. You may say to yourselves, "How can

we know when a message has not been spoken by the Lord?'' If what a prophet proclaims in the name of the Lord does not take place or come true, that is a message the Lord has not spoken. That prophet has spoken presumptuously. Do not be afraid of him.

In 1976 and 1977 over a million Jehovah's Witnesses left the Watchtower, deeply disillusioned with the organization that claimed to be the voice of God on earth, but had proven again and again to be a false prophet.

Continuation Under Franz and Henschel

Knorr, also proven to be a false prophet, died in 1977. The organization was then run by a very aged gentleman named Frederick Franz, who had been its leading theologian for over 60 years. Franz died at the end of 1992 at the age of 98. Yet the Watchtower continues to grow, now headed by 74-year-old Milton G. Henschel.

It is a rare door that hasn't felt the knock of the Jehovah's Witnesses more than once, and it is an even rarer Jehovah's Witness who has heard the gospel message at one of those doors from the resident Christian. The reason is that it is a far-from-simple task to witness to a Witness. It is easier to just close the door and avoid the difficult task of sorting through a maze of confusing doctrines. Let's try to make this task a bit simpler.

Five Important Facts

There are five important facts to remember about the Jehovah's Witnesses and the Watchtower Organization.

1. They have accepted the Organization as the prophet of God.

2. They have accepted the Organization as God's sole channel for His truth.

3. They believe that to reject the Organization is to reject God.

4. They believe that only the Organization can interpret the Bible; as individuals they are unable to do so.

5. They believe that the *Watchtower* magazine contains God's truth, directed by Him, through the Organization.

Conflict with Christianity

What does the Organization and the *Watchtower* magazine teach that is in conflict with orthodox Christianity?

1. That Jesus is a created being—a creature.

2. That Jesus is actually Michael the Archangel.

3. That Jesus was not resurrected bodily, but as a spirit being.

4. That Jesus returned invisibly in 1914 (secretly to the Organization).

5. That Jesus was only a man when on earth, not "the Word become flesh."

6. That the Holy Spirit is only an active force, not the Person of God.

7. That hell is simply the grave.

8. That heaven's doors are open to only 144,000 people.

9. That the majority of Witnesses must remain on earth.

10. That salvation is found only through the Organization.

11. That salvation can be maintained only by energetic works for the Organization until the end, when one may then merit eternal life on a paradise earth.

12. That Satan is the author of the doctrine of the trinity.

13. That Jesus cannot be given worship, but only honor as Jehovah's first creation.

Denial of the Essentials

The Jehovah's Witnesses do not believe or teach some of the very basic tenets of Christian doctrine. They deny:

1. The trinity.

2. The deity of Christ.

3. The bodily resurrection of Christ.

4. The visible return of Christ.

5. The Person of God the Holy Spirit.

6. The promise of heaven to all believers.

7. The necessity of the new birth for all believers.

8. The Lord's Supper for all believers (not only for the 144,000).

9. The eternal security of the believer.

10. The conscious eternal punishment of the lost.

The Truth from the Bible

1. **God exists in a Trinity of three eternal and co-equal persons.**

   Within the nature of the one God are three eternal Persons: Father, Son, and Holy Spirit.

   Father:

   To all in Rome who are loved by God and called to be saints: Grace and peace to you from God our Father and from the Lord Jesus Christ (Romans 1:7).

   Son:

   Thomas said to him, "My Lord and my God!" (John 20:28).

   Holy Spirit:

   Peter said, "Ananias, how is it that Satan has so filled your heart that you have lied to the Holy Spirit and have kept for yourself some of the money you received for the land? Didn't it belong to you before it was sold? And after it was sold, wasn't the money at your disposal? What made you think of doing such a thing? You have not lied to men but to God" (Acts 5:3,4).

2. **Jesus is no less than God in human flesh.**

   In Christ all the fullness of the Deity lives in bodily form (Colossians 2:9).

3. **God, the Holy Spirit, is the third member of the Holy Trinity.**

Go and make disciples of all nations, baptizing them in the name of the Father and of the Son and of the Holy Spirit (Matthew 28:19).

While they were worshiping the Lord and fasting, the Holy Spirit said, "Set apart for me Barnabas and Saul for the work to which I have called them" (Acts 13:2).

4. **Jesus Christ rose bodily from the grave.**

The Jews replied, "It has taken forty-six years to build this temple, and you are going to raise it in three days?" But the temple he had spoken of was his body (John 2:20,21).

Look at my hands and my feet. It is I myself! Touch me and see; a ghost does not have flesh and bones, as you see I have (Luke 24:39).

5. **Jesus is visibly coming again to set up His kingdom on earth.**

At that time the sign of the Son of Man will appear in the sky, and all the nations of the earth will mourn. They will see the Son of Man coming on the clouds of the sky, with power and great glory (Matthew 24:30)

You will receive power when the Holy Spirit comes on you; and you will be my witnesses in Jerusalem, and in all Judea and Samaria, and to the ends of the earth (Acts 1:8).

He is coming with the clouds, and every eye will see him, even those who pierced him; and all the peoples of the earth will mourn because of him. So shall it be! Amen (Revelation 1:7).

6. **Salvation is in the Person of Jesus Christ and comes through faith in Him.**

Believe in the Lord Jesus, and you will be saved—you and your household (Acts 16:31).

It is by grace you have been saved, through faith—and this not from yourselves, it is the gift of God—not by works, so that no one can boast (Ephesians 2:8,9).

7. **It is the work of God for man, not a work of man for God.**

When the kindness and love of God our Savior appeared, he saved us, not because of righteous things we had done, but because of his mercy. He saved us through the washing of rebirth and renewal by the Holy Spirit, whom he poured out on us generously through Jesus Christ our Savior (Titus 3:4-6).

8. **Jesus was and should be worshiped.**

A week later his disciples were in the house again, and Thomas was with them. Though the doors were locked, Jesus came and stood among them and said, "Peace be with you!" Then he said to Thomas, "Put your finger here; see my hands. Reach out your hand and put it into my side. Stop doubting and believe." Thomas said to him, "My Lord and my God!" (John 20:26-28).

When they saw the star, they were overjoyed. On coming to the house, they saw the child with his mother Mary, and they bowed down and worshiped him. Then they opened their treasures and presented him with gifts of gold and of incense and of myrrh. And having been warned in a dream not to go back to Herod, they returned to their country by another route (Matthew 2:10-12).

Those who were in the boat worshiped him, saying, "Truly you are the Son of God" (Matthew 14:33).

Witnessing to a Witness

We need to remember that anyone who denies the deity of Jesus Christ and carries the heavy burden of a false religious spirit will go through a lot of highs and lows. True believers, empowered by the companionship of God the Holy Spirit, have a constant presence of the Lord about them that seems to act like a magnet at times.

When a Watchtower member comes to your front door and you open it, what is he thinking about? What does he think when you talk about Christianity?

First, it is impossible to offer him any hope of heaven, since Jehovah's Witnesses teach and believe that only 144,000 people are going to make it to heaven, and the odds are that the visitor at your door isn't one of them.

This idea came from Joseph Franklin Rutherford, the second president. After he became president in 1917, he was prophesying that Armageddon was right around the corner. So that he could increase the membership, he began to tell his followers that only 144,000 people were going to make it to heaven.

The door-to-door crews began to tell their prospects that they had better join the Watchtower before it was too late, because Armageddon was right around the corner and the ranks of the 144,000 were filling fast.

For many years the Witnesses preached this. However, in 1935 they ran into a terrible problem. In this year the Organization grew larger than 144,000 people, heaven was filled, and Armageddon had yet to occur.

The Watchtower was in a quandary about what to do with all these extra people. Rutherford saved the day when another revelation from God came forth which said that everyone who became a Jehovah's Witness before 1935 would go to heaven. Everyone who became a Jehovah's Witness *after* 1935 would stay here on earth and live in a new paradise.

That is why when you talk to most Jehovah's Witnesses today they have absolutely no hope of ever going to heaven. They believe it because Rutherford told them so.

Twisting the Trinity

Perhaps the most cultic doctrine of the Jehovah's Witnesses is their doctrine concerning Jesus Christ and the trinity. Let us quote their own books on this subject.

> The justice of God would not permit that Jesus as a
> ransom be more than a perfect man. And certainly not

the supreme God almighty in the flesh (*Let God Be True*, page 87).

Some insist that Jesus, when on earth, was both God and man in completeness. This theory is wrong (*The Harp of God*, page 101).

The Holy Spirit is not a person and is therefore not one of the Gods of the Trinity (*Let God Be True*, page 81).

The Witnesses make a common mistake by defining the trinity as three separate Gods. However, Christianity is not polytheism. Going further, they say:

The Trinity doctrine was not conceived by Jesus or the early Christians. . . . The plain truth is that this is another of Satan's attempts to keep the God fearing person from learning the truth of Jehovah and his son Christ Jesus (*Let God Be True*, page 111).

The obvious conclusion therefore is that Satan is the originator of the Trinity doctrine (*Let God Be True*, page 101).

Concerning Jesus Christ's death and resurrection they say:

He was put to death a man, but was raised from the dead a spirit being. The man Jesus is dead, forever dead (*Studies in Scripture*, volume 5, page 45).

So the King Christ Jesus was put to death in the flesh and was resurrected an invisible spirit creature (*Let God Be True*, page 138).

How do you deal with someone who comes to your front door and brings this theology? How do you share your faith with such a person?

Answering Some Questions

Recently a pair of Jehovah's Witnesses knocked on Ron's

door. After the usual greetings, Ron invited them in on the condition that they would answer a few of his questions regarding the Jehovah's Witnesses.

They said they would be glad to answer any questions he might have. As they were sitting across the kitchen table Ron said, "I guess I really have only one question. Throughout your literature you continually say that the trinity is not taught in Scripture."

"That's right," the older of the two responded with a warm smile. "Nowhere in the Bible will you find the word 'trinity.'"

Ron countered, "The trinity is taught throughout God's Word."

"Sorry, but nowhere in the Bible will you find the word 'trinity.'"

Ron answered, "You won't find the word 'trinity,' since that's a Latin term. It means 'three in the unity of one.' It's simply a term used to describe what God has revealed to us. You use the term 'theocratic kingdom' more than any other term in your literature. Can you show me one place in the Bible where 'theocratic kingdom' is found?"

Ron continued, "If you stop using the term 'theocratic kingdom,' I'll stop using the term 'trinity.'"

The elder Witness paused before he answered. "But the trinity is not rational; you can't understand it."

"Well," Ron replied, "who told you that because you could not understand something it's not a reality? Let me ask you a question: Do you fully understand Einstein's formulation, the basis of his theory of relativity? Do you fully understand that?"

The Witnesses looked warily and silently at Ron. Ron continued, "If you tell a physics professor at the university you understand it he will probably flunk you because he doesn't understand it himself. But I can guarantee you that if an atomic bomb went off outside this building right now that you would have immediate, scientific verification of this theory whether you understand it or not."

They remained silent, so Ron continued, "The question is not what our three-pound brain can understand. The question is: What has God from His infinite eternal perspective chosen to reveal to us concerning His own nature?"

Ron paused and looked at both men. "You do believe the Bible, don't you?"

"Oh, yes, we believe the Bible," they responded.

Going to the Word

Ron was warming to the task. He replied, "That's good! Why don't we go to God's Word and see what God has to say about the trinity? Why don't you put away all your magazines and books, and I will put away all my lexicons, concordances, and dictionaries. Why don't we just go to God's Word and see what God has to say?"

Jehovah's Witnesses' main denial and stumbling block is the doctrine of the deity of Jesus Christ. For that reason we need to deal with that specifically.

There are many passages that show the clear teaching of the deity of Jesus Christ. Jehovah Witnesses love the book of Revelation more than any other book in the Bible. And since they love it so much, you might as well use it with them.

Ron brought out his Bible and smiled. "Let's begin and you will see something very interesting develop here," he promised.

Ron turned to Revelation 1:8:

> "I am the Alpha and the Omega," says the Lord God, "who is, and who was, and who is to come, the Almighty."

Ron asked, "Who is speaking here? 'I am the Alpha and Omega,' says who?" The younger man answered, "Says the Lord God, Jehovah God!"

"You are absolutely right," Ron replied. "We believe that the Alpha and Omega is Jehovah God, just as it says."

Ron continued, "Now turn to Revelation 21:5-7."

> He who was seated on the throne said, "I am making everything new!" Then he said, "Write this down, for these words are trustworthy and true." He said to

me: "It is done. I am the Alpha and the Omega, the Beginning and the End. To him who is thirsty I will give to drink without cost from the spring of the water of life. He who overcomes will inherit all this, and I will be his God and he will be my son."

"Here again we see the identification that Alpha and Omega is Jehovah God." The Watchtower visitors smiled broadly and immediately agreed with Ron. "You are absolutely right," said the elder of the two. "We believe that Alpha and Omega is Jehovah God. That's what it says."

"Now turn to Revelation 22," Ron continued, "beginning with verse 13."

> I am the Alpha and the Omega, the First and the Last, the Beginning and the End.

Again the visitors responded that these titles referred to Jehovah God, as in Revelation 1:8.

Ron continued, "There's just one more passage; do you think you could help me with it?"

"Oh," they said, "We'd be glad to." They openly smiled now as Ron appeared to grasp their understanding of Jehovah God.

Ron said, "The passage is Revelation 1:17,18. Will you read it for me?"

They turned to the verse in their Watchtower Bible and the elder one began to read.

> When I saw him, I fell at his feet as though dead. Then he placed his right hand on me and said: "Do not be afraid. I am the First and the Last" (Revelation 1:17).

Ron said, "Stop. I've been trying to figure out who the First and the Last is. Tell me who he is."

They replied, "We just saw who the First and the Last is. The First and the Last is Alpha and Omega, Jehovah God."

Ron asked, "You mean to tell me the First and the Last is Jehovah God?"

They replied, "Of course he's Jehovah God."
Ron answered, "Well, keep reading."

> I am the Living One; I was dead, and behold I am
> alive for ever and ever! And I hold the keys of death
> and Hades (Revelation 1:18).

The Silence of Defeat

There was a hush that followed. Ron then asked, *"When did Jehovah die? When did God die?"* There was no answer as the men stared silently into their Scriptures.

Finally the man who did most of the talking said, "I've never seen *that* before."

"Well," Ron answered, "Is this your own Bible you are using, published by the Watchtower?"

He said, "Well, yes, but I've never seen that before."

Ron asked, "So tell me—when did Jehovah die?" They just kept looking at the verse.

At last they quietly answered, "But Jesus died."

Ron said, "Oh, you mean Jesus is Jehovah God?"

They replied, "Well, no. He can't be."

"Why not?" Ron asked.

"Well, if Jesus *is* Jehovah God, that would change everything else in the Bible—everything else we believe about him."

"You know, that's what I thought too," Ron answered.

The older man stood. "We have to leave now."

Ron said, "Sir, could you find out for me when Jehovah died? Would you go back to your Kingdom Hall and ask your overseer when Jehovah died? When you get the answer, could you bring your Watchtower leaders back to my house so they could tell me? I would really appreciate that." Needless to say, they never returned.

Every Knee Shall Bow

Jesus Christ was 100 percent God and also 100 percent man. The Jehovah's Witnesses can deal with the humanity of Christ, but will not submit to His deity. Where does that leave them? The apostle Paul helps clarify this point for us.

Your attitude should be the same as that of Christ Jesus: Who, being in very nature God, did not consider equality with God something to be grasped, but made himself nothing, taking the very nature of a servant, being made in human likeness. And being found in appearance as a man, he humbled himself and became obedient to death—even death on a cross! Therefore God exalted him to the highest place and gave him the name that is above every name, that at the name of Jesus every knee should bow, in heaven and on earth and under the earth, and every tongue confess that Jesus Christ is Lord, to the glory of God the Father (Philippians 2:5-11).

Paul is telling us that though Jesus Christ is eternally God by nature, He did not cling to his prerogative as God's equal, but chose to humble Himself and take on human flesh. Christ did not give up His divine nature. But while on earth Jesus Christ chose to temporarily self-impose limitations upon His divine attributes.

While on earth, Jesus Christ chose not to be omniscient. He chose not to be omnipotent, and He chose rather to live as a man and to submit himself fully to the will of the Father on earth. When He died on the cross He was the perfect sacrifice, the infinite sacrifice, the eternal lamb of God who shed His blood once for all time for the remission of our sins.

One day every single person, including every person who has perpetuated gross heresy about Christ, will have to meet the Master. On that day every knee shall bow, in heaven and on earth and under the earth, and every tongue shall confess that Jesus Christ is Lord, to the glory of God the Father.

Whether it is at the banqueting table of joy in heaven or at the Great White Throne judgment of the damned, *every knee shall bow.*

We thank God for Jesus Christ, who took our sin and nailed it to the cross, covering it with His shed blood as the infinite payment. We thank the Lord for the Holy Spirit, who comes and lives in us and gives us new life. To God be the honor and glory and praise!

9

Fast Facts on

Jesus and the Cults

It's not like we should have been surprised. Jesus talked about it and the disciples asked questions about it. It's there in the Word for us to read and study.

> As Jesus was sitting on the Mount of Olives, the disciples came to him privately. "Tell us," they said, "when will this happen, and what will be the sign of your coming and of the end of the age?" Jesus answered: "Watch out that no one deceives you. For many will come in my name, claiming, 'I am the Christ, ' and will deceive many." You will hear of wars and rumors of wars, but see to it that you are not alarmed. Such things must happen, but the end is still to come. Nation will rise against nation, and kingdom against kingdom. There will be famines and earthquakes in various places. All these are the beginning of birth pains (Matthew 24:3-8).

Jesus told His disciples that His coming would be in the midst of a time when many false Christs would be deceiving many people. Yet many people are still asking that same question today: How are we to know when Jesus Christ will return? What will be the signs of the second coming?

Jesus promised that He would return, and He gave some clues about that return.

In 1984 and 1985 Ron and his family were living as missionaries in the Philippine Islands. During those two years he spoke throughout the country, traveling among its many islands. He would often share a story with the Filipino people that they all remembered.

I Shall Return!

Most people do not realize that simultaneously with the bombing of Pearl Harbor on December 7, 1941, the Japanese were also bombing Clark Air Force Base north of Manila. General Douglas MacArthur, who was stationed in Manila at the time, was forced to leave the islands and fly down to Australia to assist in the allied war plan for the South Pacific.

But MacArthur radioed back a stirring message to the people of the Philippines: "I shall return!" As Ron puts it, "If you talk to the Filipinos who lived during the Second World War, they will tell you that they lived for those words. They knew that if MacArthur promised 'I shall return,' he would keep that promise." In 1944 MacArthur fulfilled that promise and liberated the Philippine Islands.

So also our Lord Jesus Christ has said, "I shall return." But His disciples wanted to know the *signs* of the second coming. Reading these Scriptures is like reading today's newspaper as it talks about wars and rumors of wars of nation against nation, and as it talks about earthquakes and famines in many places. Notice that Jesus listed the rising up of false Christs as the number-one sign of the last days.

Twice more in that same discussion with His disciples, Jesus returned to the same theme. In Matthew 24:11 He stated, "Many false prophets will appear and deceive many people." As He closed His remarks He again said:

> At that time if anyone says to you, "Look, here is the Christ!" or, "There he is!" do not believe it. For false Christs and false prophets will appear and perform great signs and miracles to deceive even the elect—if that were possible. See, I have told you ahead of time (Matthew 24:23-25).

We are seeing the fulfillment of those warnings today as never before. For example, recently the Reverend Sun

Myung Moon, founder of the Unification Church, held a conference in San Francisco in which he declared that he was the Messiah and that he is the second coming of Jesus Christ.

When you study the history of cults in America, you realize that 150 years ago we had just a few thousand people in the cults. But now we have a thousand different *cults*, with some 25 to 30 million adherents, and the number is still growing. There has been a literal explosion of false Christs and false prophets.

Testing the Teachers

There is a way to test these false Christs and false teachers. The Word of God states:

> All Scripture is God-breathed and is useful for teaching, rebuking, correcting and training in righteousness, so that the man of God may be thoroughly equipped for every good work (2 Timothy 3:16,17).

In chapter 4 of the same letter, Paul exhorts us:

> In the presence of God and of Christ Jesus, who will judge the living and the dead, and in view of his appearing and his kingdom, I give you this charge: Preach the Word; be prepared in season and out of season; correct, rebuke and encourage—with great patience and careful instruction. For the time will come when men will not put up with sound doctrine. Instead, to suit their own desires, they will gather around them a great number of teachers to say what their itching ears want to hear. They will turn their ears away from the truth and turn aside to myths (2 Timothy 4:1-4).

We are seeing this phenomenon today as never before. People are turning from sound doctrine and the truth of God's words to every type of man-made Christ, myth, and aberration.

The term "cult" really came to many people's attention for the first time in November 1978. The newspapers told a story of unbelievable horror. The headlines that flashed all over the world said, "913 Americans Commit Mass Suicide at Jonestown, Guyana."

Time magazine told the story of the "cult of death," about a man named Jim Jones, who had begun as a legitimate Christian minister in Indiana. He came to San Francisco and set himself up as the voice of God on earth. He started what he called "The People's Temple" and eventually led his followers to Guyana in South America.

There he claimed to be Jesus Christ Himself. He so convinced those people that he was God's voice on earth that when he told them to take Dixie cups and dip them into a vat of grape Flavoraid laced with poison, 900 Americans dipped their cups into that vat, gave the poison to their babies and their children, and then drank it themselves.

The cover of *Newsweek* magazine that week showed the bloated bodies of the 900 Americans lying in the tropical jungle in South America. People said, "I can't believe it! How could it happen? How could 900 Americans follow a man and commit mass suicide?"

The commander of the U.S. forces who was responsible for going to Jonestown, cleaning the camp out, and bringing the bodies back for burial was a Christian. When he returned with the bodies to Dover Air Force Base he held a press conference. We'll never forget one of the things he said: "The thing that interested me most about Jonestown is that when we cleaned the camp out, we did not find a single Bible in all of Jonestown."

Jim Jones had so effectively replaced the Bible with his own man-made teaching and theology, he had so convinced those people that he was God's voice on earth, that when he told them to drink poison, they did it. If you believe that some man or organization is the voice of God, the prophet of God on earth, who are you to question the voice of God on earth?

We want to give you a brief overview of the cults in this

chapter. There are actually four categories of cults preva-
lent today in America. These are:

1. Pseudo-Christian cults.

2. Oriental cults.

3. New Age cults.

4. Spiritist cults or the occult.

Pseudo-Christian Cults

Over the last 150 years the classical definition of a cult
has referred to this first category as the pseudo-Christian
cults. These are religious organizations or movements that
claim to be Christian and claim to believe in the Bible. But
instead of building their theology and teaching on God's
Word, the Bible, they claim some "new revelation" or man-
made teaching as superior to the Bible. By interpreting the
Bible through the grid of their particular revelation or
teaching, these groups end up denying the central doctrines of historic, orthodox, biblical Christianity. The key
perversions of the cults always relate to the central issues of
theology, specifically the doctrines of God, Jesus Christ,
and salvation.

These groups are considered cults because they seek to
counterfeit biblical Christianity. Counterfeits deceive by
their outward appearance. Like counterfeit money, the
cults want to look and sound like the genuine thing without
having their bogus nature detected. This is precisely what
deceives so many people when confronted by one of the
above groups. Such cults use Christian terminology to
sound Christian, but then redefine the terms to fit their
own man-made theology.

The definition of terms is key to understanding the cult
deception. To illustrate the point, take a jar of mayonnaise
out of the refrigerator and empty the jar of all of its contents. Then replace the contents with Crisco shortening.
Screw the lid back on and put the jar back into the refrigerator. The next person who goes to get a spoonful of

mayonnaise will see a jar that says "mayonnaise," but when he eats it, it will make him choke!

The pseudo-Christian cults have essentially emptied biblical Christianity of all of its content theologically. They have replaced the content with a perverted theology of their own making, then sprayed it over with Christian words and terminology to make it look and sound Christian. Now they market it as a new revelation from God. Many people naively buy the outer wrapping without first examining the content and essence of the package. This can be deadly to your spiritual health and ultimate eternal destiny!

Such organizations include the Watchtower Bible and Tract Society (known as the Jehovah's Witnesses) and the Church of Jesus Christ of Latter-Day Saints (known as the Mormons). Also included are Mary Baker Eddy and her group (known as Christian Science), as well as the *Plain Truth* magazine, and the Worldwide Church of God in Pasadena, California.

There are other groups as well, such as the Unification Church, The Way International, Unity, and many other organizations. All of these claim to be Christian and claim to believe the Bible, but instead of building their teaching from what God has revealed, they claim some new revelation and some man-made teaching which they say supersedes the Bible.

These groups interpret the Bible through their own revelations or teaching and end up denying the basic doctrines and central beliefs of historic biblical Christianity. They use the term "Jesus Christ" but redefine the term to fit their own theology.

For example, if you go to a Christian Science Reading Room and ask, "Do you believe in the trinity?" the adherents will reply, "Of course we do!" But if you ask them, "What is the trinity?" they will tell you the trinity is three ethical principles: life, truth, and love. In other words, they use Christian words to make you think they are Christian, and then redefine those words to fit their own theology.

If you ask a Mormon missionary, "Do you believe in Jesus Christ?" he will reply, "Of course. I'm wearing a little name tag here that says that we are the Church of Jesus Christ." But if you ask that Mormon who Jesus Christ actually is, you will find that they believe that Jesus Christ is the brother of Lucifer and that he is simply one God in a pantheon of Gods. Mormons are polytheists; they believe there are millions of Gods. They deny the Virgin Birth and teach that Christ was born through physical sex between God, who is a physical man, and Mary.

It is the same story, with slightly different details, for each of the cults. Their Jesus looks like the real Jesus only on the surface. Dig a little and another one of those false Christs rises up. In dealing with the cults, *you must define your terminology.* What do you mean when you talk about God? What do you mean when you talk about Jesus Christ? What do you mean when you talk about salvation?

Oriental Cults

A second category of cults is the Oriental cults. These are the cults that have their basis in Oriental or Eastern philosophy, specifically Hinduism and Buddhism. They include the Hare Krishna movement (or Krishna consciousness), the Divine Light Mission, Transcendental Meditation, Yoga, Zen, and many others. It is interesting to note that while all the American cults are going to Asia, the Asian cults are coming to America!

All the Oriental cults basically teach a Hindu pantheism: that we are all part of an impersonal universe which they call God. They say people suffer in life because they think they are personal beings. In Hinduism and Buddhism personal thinking and feeling is an illusion. The world is also an illusion, and in order to get rid of suffering we must get rid of the physical, personal world, which is not real. We must transcend it through Transcendental Meditation or Yoga meditation to become part of the impersonal universe.

We need to understand something: An "impersonal universe" never loved or cared about anyone. *Only a personal*

Creator loves and cares for His creation. The world at large is lost to that simple theology. They want the answer to be within their control, within their understanding, within themselves. And the false gods they play with like it that way.

New Age Cults

The New Age cults are sometimes referred to as the Human Potential movement. These groups combine Eastern philosophy with Western humanism and mix it with the occult to teach that man has evolved physically as an animal in the first stage of life. They say we are standing on the brink of a New Age, the Age of Aquarius, and that in this New Age man will continue his evolution spiritually to achieve his own divine nature.

The New Age movement combines three major philosophies into a new holistic worldview which is expected to usher in the next century and the Age of Aquarius.

The New Age movement combines the following elements:

Western Secular Humanism:

♦ No personal God or Creator
♦ Evolution
♦ Man supreme
♦ Man basically good
♦ Human potential to become god

Eastern Hindu Mysticism:

♦ Pantheism
♦ We are one with nature
♦ We are part of impersonal cosmos
♦ Yoga, TM
♦ Reincarnation

The Occult:

♦ Spiritism
♦ Channeling
♦ Spirit guides
♦ Astrology

♦ Crystals
♦ Tapping into cosmic forces

The New Age movement combines these philosophies to form the ultimate rebellion against God, the Creator. Man wants to save himself and become God himself in the New Age. This movement is empowered by "deceiving spirits and things taught by demons" (1 Timothy 4:1).

Becoming God is the oldest lie recorded in the Bible. In the Garden of Eden, the serpent said to Adam and Eve, "Eat of the fruit. You can become God yourselves." Isn't it interesting that Satan hasn't changed? He's still promoting that same old lie that he dresses up in new terms and pawns off as new revelation.

This is the cry of the cults from New Age to Mormonism: "You can become God yourself!" It's the ultimate lie, the ultimate sin—man wanting to become God himself.

But because people do not find what they are looking for in their own divinity, many of them have gone into a fourth category, the spiritist cults.

Spiritist Cults

This category of cults spans the whole universe of darkness, including astrology, tarot cards, palmistry, numerology, witchcraft, Satanism, seances, clairvoyance, and channeling.

Paul warned us that in the last days before Christ returns at His second coming, we would see the rise of such evil.

> The Spirit clearly says that in later times some will abandon the faith and follow deceiving spirits and things taught by demons (1 Timothy 4:1).

We are certainly seeing the fulfillment of that Scripture today, in the decade of the 1990's, as never before.

Probably no Scripture centers more on these practices than the book of Deuteronomy.

> When you enter the land the Lord your God is giving you, do not learn to imitate the detestable ways

of the nations there. Let no one be found among you who sacrifices his son or daughter in the fire, who practices divination or sorcery, interprets omens, engages in witchcraft, or casts spells, or who is a medium or spiritist or who consults the dead. Anyone who does these things is detestable to the Lord, and because of these detestable practices the Lord your God will drive out those nations before you. You must be blameless before the Lord your God. The nations you will dispossess listen to those who practice sorcery or divination. But as for you, the Lord your God has not permitted you to do so (Deuteronomy 18:9-14).

Jude 3 tells us to contend for the faith which was once for all entrusted to the saints. That is what we must do in dealing with the cults. Paul warned the church in Corinth of these very dangers.

I am jealous for you with a godly jealousy. I promised you to one husband, to Christ, so that I might present you as a pure virgin to him. But I am afraid that just as Eve was deceived by the serpent's cunning, your minds may somehow be led astray from your sincere and pure devotion to Christ. For if someone comes to you and preaches a Jesus other than the Jesus we preached, or if you receive a different spirit from the one you received, or a different gospel from the one you accepted, you put up with it easily enough. For such men are false apostles, deceitful workmen, masquerading as apostles of Christ. And no wonder, for Satan himself masquerades as an angel of light. It is not surprising, then, if his servants masquerade as servants of righteousness. Their end will be what their actions deserve (2 Corinthians 11:2-4,13-15).

Paul emphasized that *your minds may somehow be led astray.* He is saying, "I am afraid for you Christians because there's going to come another Jesus, another gospel, another spirit—counterfeits brought to you by false apostles who are disguising themselves to look like Christians. So don't be surprised, since even Satan disguised himself as an angel of light."

What is on top of the Mormon Temple in Salt Lake City? At the highest pinnacle there is Moroni, the angel of light, who told Joseph Smith that all the teachings of Christianity are an abomination, and that he could become God himself.

It is interesting to note how many cults began by somebody getting a revelation from an angel of light. One billion people today are following Islam because a man named Muhammad claimed to have received revelations from an angel of light, who told him that Jesus Christ was not God, that Jesus Christ did not die on a cross for man's sins, and that man can save himself by keeping the law of Muhammad.

The Jesus of the Cults

There is a veritable smorgasbord of Jesus Christs being served up to the public today. Jesus warned of this and so did Paul, and we've got them by the hundreds today! (By the millions if you believe Shirley MacLaine's pronouncement that we are all Jesus Christs!)

Who is the Jesus of Jehovah's Witnesses? He is the archangel Michael. He was the first creation of God, he came to earth as a man, he died on a stake, and he rose invisibly as a ghost.

The Mormons say that Jesus was simply one god in a pantheon of gods. He is the brother of Satan, and the cross and blood of Christ are foolishness.

Mary Baker Eddy taught in Christian Science that Jesus was just a pleasant divine idea.

Herbert W. Armstrong, founder of the Worldwide Church of God, says that Jesus was the first man to self-perfect himself and is now our example of how we can perfect ourselves by membership in Armstrong's church (by tithing up to 30 percent of our income to them).

Sun Myung Moon and the Unification Church say that Jesus was a man who failed, and that Sun Myung Moon is the second coming of Jesus Christ.

The Bahais say that Jesus is one of nine great world manifestations. They say it does not matter what religion you believe, since all religions are basically the same.

The Bahai Temple in Evanston, Illinois, is nine-sided, with each side representing one of the world's religions. They say it doesn't matter which door you come in, since all religions are basically the same. Big signs on the walls read, "All religions teach the same thing about God."

The Unitarians say that Jesus was a good man but his followers mistakenly deified him.

The spiritists say that Jesus is an advanced medium in the sixth sphere in the astrological projection.

The Rosicrucians say that Jesus is a manifestation of cosmic consciousness.

Maharishi and Transcendental Meditation say that Jesus was an enlightened guru who never suffered or died for anyone.

The Jesus of the cults is not the Jesus of the Bible. They have another Jesus, a counterfeit, a false Christ who can save no one.

Knowing the Real Jesus

Who is the real Jesus Christ? That is the ultimate question.

> Dear friends, do not believe every spirit, but test the spirits to see whether they are from God, because many false prophets have gone out into the world.
>
> This is how you can recognize the Spirit of God: Every spirit that acknowledges that Jesus Christ has come in the flesh is from God, but every spirit that does not acknowledge Jesus is not from God. This is the spirit of the antichrist, which you have heard is coming and even now is already in the world (1 John 4:1-3).

John says to test these people. Do they confess that Jesus Christ has come in the flesh? If they deny that fact, then they are of the antichrist. Many cults believe that their particular Jesus was "in the flesh," but John had already recorded for us in his Gospel who this unique One was who had come in the flesh.

John starts his gospel with a clear statement that God took on human flesh and became God incarnate.

> In the beginning was the Word, and the Word was with God, and *the Word was God.*
>
> *The Word became flesh* and made his dwelling among us. We have seen his glory, the glory of the One and Only, who came from the Father, full of grace and truth (John 1:1,14).

The cults have another gospel, one which will enslave you into a man-made system as you try to earn your salvation apart from Jesus Christ. But Jesus Christ Himself is the way, the truth, and the life. No one comes to the Father but by him (John 14:6).

Acts 4:12 says, "There is no other name under heaven given among men by which we must be saved" (NKJV). Salvation is not a man-made system or organization, but it is a gift of God. It was bought and paid for by the eternal Lamb of God, Jesus Christ, who was the infinite sacrifice. He shed His blood on the cross for an infinite amount of sins so that we could come by faith and receive His free gift of salvation. That's why we call it "good news." It is the true power of God Himself available to each and every one of us.

10

The Korean Messiah: Sun Myung Moon and the Unification Church

The August 17, 1990, headline in the *San Francisco Chronicle* read "Rev. Moon Says He's The Messiah." The article stated, "Surrounding himself with an eclectic collection of swamis, scholars, lamas, and imams, the Rev. Sun Myung Moon yesterday declared himself the new world messiah!"

Moon, the controversial Korean founder of the Unification Church, made his pronouncement at the opening session of his Assembly of the World Religious, a lavish, all-expenses-paid conference that Moon is bankrolling at the San Francisco Airport Hyatt Regency.

Moon said the world needs to find its "true parent" and free itself from Satan's influence. "This person is the messiah," said Moon. "To help fulfill this very purpose, I have been called upon by God."

According to Unification Church doctrine, Jesus failed in His mission and must be supplanted by a second, Korean-born messiah.

Question and Answer

In Matthew 24, the disciples came to Jesus and asked Him a question that was perplexing them. As He was sitting on the Mount of Olives, the disciples came to Him privately saying, "When will these thing be? And what will be the sign of Your coming and of the end of the age?" (verse 3 NKJV).

Those same questions have been on the minds of many people today. We still want to know when Jesus will return. We still wonder what will be the signs of the second coming of Jesus Christ.

Jesus answered His disciples' question by saying:

> Watch out that no one deceives you. For many will come in my name, claiming, "I am the Christ," and will deceive many (Matthew 24:4,5).

> At that time many will turn away from the faith and will betray and hate each other, and many false prophets will appear and deceive many people (Matthew 24:10,11).

> At that time if anyone says to you, "Look, here is the Christ!" or, "There he is!" do not believe it. For false Christs and false prophets will appear and perform great signs and miracles to deceive even the elect—if that were possible. See, I have told you ahead of time. So if anyone tells you, "There he is, out in the desert," do not go out; or, "Here he is, in the inner rooms," do not believe it. For as lightning that comes from the east is visible even in the west, so will be the coming of the Son of Man. Wherever there is a carcass, there the vultures will gather (Matthew 24:23-28).

Three times in His discourse concerning the last days before He returns, Jesus warned us that in the last days there would come many false Christs and false prophets. Powerful deceivers would lead many people astray.

We are seeing this phenomenon today on an unprecedented scale. We are seeing cults and new religious personalities rising up as never before. Perhaps it is the advent of the electronic age we live in, but more likely it is because we are moving with lightning speed toward the end of the age as described by Christ Himself.

In this chapter we will deal with one of the most obvious

of the false prophets, one who epitomizes the classic characteristics of false prophets who claim to be the Christ.

Seeing the Sources

The Reverend Sun Myung Moon imparts the secrets of his divinity and theology in two major sources. One is *The Divine Principle*, which is his sacred book, published in 1967. The other is found in a work known as *The Master Speaks*, in which are published sermons that he has given. This book is sent out to the Moon centers around the world.

In order to understand that Sun Myung Moon is truly one of those foretold by Christ, we need to look at the text of some of his own lectures.

> I am the incarnation of God, the whole world is in my hands, and I will conquer and subjugate the world. God is now throwing Christianity away and is now establishing a new religion, and this new religion is the Unification Church. All the Christians in the world are destined to be absorbed by our movement.
>
> There have been saints, prophets, many religious leaders in past human history. But Master Moon here, is more than any of those people, and greater than Jesus himself. . . . I am a thinker, I am your brain. When you join the effort with me, you can do everything in utter obedience to me, because what I am doing is not done at random, but what I am doing is under God's command. There is no complaint or objection against anything being done here until we have established the Kingdom of God on earth. Up until the very end there can never be any complaints!
>
> I want to have the members under me who will be willing to obey me even though they may have to disobey their own parents and the presidents of their own nations. And if I gain half the population of the world, I can turn the whole world upside down (as quoted in *Time*, June 14, 1976).

Moon is not a run-of-the-mill prophet or dictator. Moon is here to establish a one-world unification, and he as the direct representation of God is going to rule that unified world.

Moon's great work, from his own mouth, is "to build the Kingdom of God on earth." He claims, "The whole world is in my hands, and I will conquer and subjugate the world."

This new kingdom will not be Jewish, Muslim, or Christian. It will not be Korean or American, but it will be a one-world religion and a one-world government under Moon's total control. This is his divine mission and that of every adherent to the Unification faith.

During the American Bicentennial, Moon held a huge rally in Yankee Stadium in New York City, where he proclaimed he was going to initiate the New Age and the Kingdom of God.

He began his sermon that day by saying:

> Ladies and gentlemen, if there is illness in your home, do you not need a doctor from outside? God has sent me to America in the role of a doctor and in the role of a firefighter. For the last three years, with my entire heart and soul I have been teaching American youth a new revelation from God.

The New Revelation

We need to examine not only who Sun Myung Moon is, but this new revelation which Moon claims to be teaching to American youth.

In Galatians, Paul talked about the coming of Sun Myung Moon.

> I am astonished that you are so quickly deserting the one who called you by the grace of Christ and are turning to a different gospel—which is really no gospel at all. Evidently some people are throwing you into confusion and are trying to pervert the gospel of Christ. But even if we or an angel from heaven should preach a gospel other than the one we preached to you, let him be eternally condemned! As we have already said, so now I say again: If anybody is preaching

to you a gospel other than what you accepted, let him be eternally condemned! (Galatians 1:6-9).

Paul used the strongest Greek term possible—*Anathema: under the divine curse.* Sun Myung Moon is bringing a new revelation, a false gospel. As we are going to see, it is a curse in God's eyes.

Sun Myung Moon claims that his organization, known as the Unification Church, has a worldwide membership of around 600,000. Most of these people are in Korea and Japan, although he claims to have over 30,000 members in the United States as well.

Although that is not a very large number, the "Moonies" have gained great notoriety in the national press because of their soliciting on street corners and at airports. The Unification Church now has strong financial power and great public-relations clout.

Moon and his followers have bought the New Yorker Hotel, right across from Madison Square Garden. They use it as their international headquarters. They are also deeply involved in political activities in Washington D.C., and they own and publish the Washington *Times* newspaper.

Of the 30,000 Americans who are followers of Sun Myung Moon, about 7000 to 10,000 are hard-core, full-time members who are out working on the streets 18 to 20 hours a day, soliciting funds and new converts.

Sun Myung Moon is a multimillionaire, with assets of over 30 million dollars in South Korea, 20 million dollars in Japan, and over 30 million dollars in the United States. He has gained his wealth through a variety of manufacturing enterprises, producing cosmetics, rifles, instant tea, titanium, and pharmaceuticals, and more.

In the last few years Sun Myung Moon has been buying up much of the commercial fishing industry in the United States. This has become a great concern to the fishing industry as he continues to acquire canneries and fishing fleets along the Gulf of Mexico, the Eastern Seaboard, the West Coast, and Alaska.

In an average year, Moonies selling flowers, candy, and peanuts on street corners take in close to 20 million tax-free dollars. In New York State alone they own over 25 million dollars in property.

How It All Began

How did this all begin? How did Moon reach this pinnacle of power? Sun Myung Moon was born in the 1920's in North Korea. He claims that on Easter morning in 1936, Jesus appeared to him and told him he was chosen to complete the "unfinished task" of Christ.

Moon's entire theology rests on the belief that Jesus Christ failed in His mission and that Sun Myung Moon was chosen to complete the "unfinished task." Moon claims to have been a clairvoyant and spiritist from birth. He claims he has been in regular contact with Buddha, Krishna, Jesus, Moses, and a variety of other prophets.

For these claims and for his theology Moon was excommunicated by the Presbyterian Church in Korea in 1948. But in 1954 he established his own church, called the Holy Spirit Association for the Unification of World Christianity. He then shortened this to the Unification Church. In 1957 Sun Myung Moon published *The Divine Principle*, which is his 500-page interpretation of the Bible.

In 1970 Moon started his work in the United States, and it expanded so rapidly that he moved its headquarters to the New Yorker Hotel.

What Is the Attraction?

People often ask, "How does somebody ever get involved with Sun Myung Moon? What is it that attracts young people to get involved in such an organization and spend 18 hours a day raising funds on street corners, seeking new converts, sleeping only four hours a night, and being continually moved about like vagabonds?"

Moon and his recruiters usually look for two types of individuals. First, they go on university campuses and look for that lonely person—the young freshman girl who is sitting alone, who is away from home for the first time, who appears to have no friends. They walk up to her and befriend her.

To a lonely person on a big university campus, anybody who will accept her and befriend her is a welcome sight. They invite her to a dinner, where they do what is known as "love-bombing."

In love-bombing, the Moonies saturate a person with friendship and acceptance, telling her (or him) how important she is and how much they love her. Of course, this feeds on the person's desire to be accepted and needed. Then, if the recruit will come with them to a weekend retreat, they begin the real indoctrination into the cult.

The second type of individual that the Moonies seek to recruit is the idealistic person who wants to build a Utopia on earth.

Time magazine published the testimony of a girl named Cynthia who was involved in the Moon organization. She related a very typical rendition of how she got involved.

Cynthia said she had seen a blind advertisement in the *Denver Post* that read, "Sincere, conscientious person interested in the betterment of mankind, call this number." Out of curiosity she called, and the young woman who answered explained that she worked for an organization similar to the Peace Corps that operated out of the community center in Boulder, Colorado. She asked Cynthia to come in for an interview.

> The Center was located across from the University of Colorado in the old Chi Omega sorority house. I talked with a young man from Austria and he told me he belonged to a youth movement and asked me if I would like to come to a weekend retreat to learn more about it. I really liked the attitude in the place, and little did I know that my mind had begun a journey from which it may never return.
>
> Starting at 9:00 A.M. on Saturday, a group of about fifteen of us heard lectures lasting all day long. That night we were told that the end of the world was at hand, and before this, the second coming of Christ would occur. We were also told that the person who had brought these new truths to the world was Sun Myung Moon, a Korean. When I wanted to leave, I was told that Satan would try to pull me away from

God because I had been chosen to build the kingdom of heaven. I felt that someone had placed a psychological bomb in my head, and if I left, it would explode.

That week, I was driven to spend a few days on a farm in [a small town in] Oklahoma. We heard lectures every day and then worked and sang in the yard. We all ended up the week by joining and then went back to our own centers.

When I arrived in Boulder, I was allowed to go into the prayer room to see Moon's picture. We prayed out loud for 20 minutes, heard a leader read from Moon's works, sang songs, and bowed before Moon's picture. Moon and his wife, we were taught, were the true parents of mankind.

The schedule was always the same: up before the sunrise, breakfast with more songs and prayers, and then fund-raising. We all went in vans to towns around Boulder, singing and praying. Even if we could only wrangle a penny from somebody, it was a victory for God. The more money we raised, the more God-centered we were. We even had to go to bars at night to raise money, arriving home anywhere between 11:30 and 1:00 A.M.

After two weeks of this, I was so tired that, as I arose in the morning, I would fall against the wall. In five weeks of fund-raising, I raised over 3000 dollars for the organization (*Time* magazine, June 14, 1976).

Young, idealistic people are very attracted to the Moonies' claims and will go on what seems to be a kind of weekend retreat to learn more about them. Without realizing it, they fall prey to a planned system, a gradual process of indoctrination and brainwashing.

Their mentors continually pound in their heads the idea that the world is of Satan, that Sun Myung Moon has brought the truth, and that they are chosen to be a part of that new kingdom.

The peer pressure is increased in proportion to the group acceptance, and then the recruit is put into isolation and kept awake 20 hours at a time, producing an exhaustion designed to gradually tear the mind and personality.

Throughout the exhaustion, the recruit is given a low-protein diet that increases this mental breakdown. Over a period of days the recruit's mental resistance is gradually broken down while the Moonies instill, through a continuous, repetitious chanting, the philosophy and teaching of Sun Myung Moon. The recruit becomes literally enslaved to the Moon organization.

Agony in a Diary

Another former Moonie shared part of her diary, which she kept while she was in the Moon organization, with the readers of *Seventeen* magazine in 1976. It was a heart-wrenching picture.

> Like thousands of Moonies across the country, I worked all day every day, selling carnations, to raise money for the movement. Up at 4:00 A.M., rattling through the streets with other teens in a seatless van by 5:00, heading for shopping centers or business districts. Breakfast was Chinese rice balls or cereal and candy served in the van, with milk spilling all over.
>
> Team Captains whip us up into evangelical frenzy with songs, Bible verses, prayers and chants until we shout out, in determination, the amount we will personally raise that day. No one shouts out an amount less than 100 dollars. Some caught up in the moment scream "one thousand dollars!" On the streets till the money is made no matter how long it takes; rarely back before midnight or 1:00 A.M. Dinner is vegetables, starches, no meat.
>
> Sometimes we are so tired we don't even eat. Testimonies then about interesting experiences of the day, with emphasis on visions and mystical revelation of Reverend Moon, more Bible, more drumming about Moon, more singing to drive away the evil spirits. We collapse and sleep until the next day begins before dawn.
>
> All emotion, everything is handled by the Center Director. If I sing too loud, he tells me how to sing. If I want to eat or sit with different people, he says "no." If I feel like

crying, he says don't cry for yourself. We have no newspapers, no TV, no radio and no talk of the outside world. Only later, after I had left the cult, did I see what was happening here. The warm kids in New York fear showing any emotion because they have been made to believe that negative thoughts are a sign that the devil has invaded them. They are under great pressure to win new recruits like me so the day will be blessed by Reverend Moon.

Now, though I do not realize it yet, I am being manipulated in another way. The lack of sleep, the poor food, the ceaseless noise and commotion, the isolation, the chanted prayers and songs weaken my resolution and make me desperately afraid of trying to break free. I never wake without wondering what I am doing here, but by the time the determinations are hollered out, I am thinking only of how to sell enough flowers to meet my quota. If we don't sell more, the Captain says Reverend Moon will fail to win this country, and Satan will triumph.

Like the others, I lie. The money goes for drug rehabilitation programs, I tell some people, or for Christian youth projects. Few ask for details. Sun Myung Moon says it is okay to lie to achieve your goal; he calls it heavenly deceit. The flowers sell for donations of at least one dollar apiece, triple their cost. Some days I raise over $240.00, but never less than one hundred. I give it all to the Captains and never hear of it again. We're on the road now. My legs ache from pounding the pavement. An inch-thick callous has hardened on my sole. I am sick with fever. I can't get up. Other Moonies sprinkle holy salt around my bed to drive away bad spirits. A doctor? Forget it.

I know of one Moon girl who developed an eye ailment. Other members were brought to see her writhing in pain, as an example of someone who had been possessed. By the time she was finally allowed to get medical treatment, she was partially blind. If you are sick, it means your ancestors sinned, and you are paying for it.

September, 1974—I am physically and emotionally drained. I am back in New York for a new assignment witnessing and winning new converts. My days, rain or shine, are spent approaching people as I was first approached at the library. I don't have a knack for spotting good prospects, as some Moonies do. Day after day, people ignore me. I am swept with guilt and fears.

The Center Director tells me if I witness unsuccessfully to a girl, and next week she is raped, it is my fault because I didn't bring her into the movement. I am given conditions or punishments that free me from Satan's influences: cold showers, longer and longer ones, reading Moon's doctrine over and over, praying all night long in repentance, begging God to forgive me, fasting a week at a time. By eagerly serving the conditions, I can overcome my sins. Oh, God, please help me. I am so afraid.

Most people do not fully understand such intense brain-washing, but the tactics that Sun Myung Moon uses are very similar to those which some of the prisoners of war underwent in North Korea during the Korean War.

Moon is producing an army of adolescents in adult bodies, and they are simply programmed to respond to whatever Moon asks them to do. He is seeking to create unity without diversity. Everybody is totally submitted to his will.

That is the opposite of what we have in the Christian church. The New Testament teaches that in unity we may have diversity. But Moon teaches that we must have unity *without* diversity, even if it produces a robot world.

The Four-Point Program

Researchers have done studies on how young people get attracted to such cults. They have found that for a person to become established as a mature individual in life, four things must occur.

First, a person must establish independence from his or her family in order to become a confident individual. Second, a person needs to know how to relate successfully to people of the opposite sex. Third, a person must prepare for an occupation to support himself. Fourth, a mature person must establish a meaningful and workable philosophy of life.

Psychologists say that many of the cults are fulfilling those four functions for young people today. In the first requirement, people become independent from their families by becoming dependent upon the cults and cult leaders. We saw this graphically portrayed in Jonestown. Jim Jones had become the father figure, the authoritarian leader requiring total dependence on him. The frightening thing is that what we see going on in the Unification Church is very close to what Jim Jones did in seeking to totally control people.

Second, the cults are instructing people in how to relate to the opposite sex by giving them a strict code of moral ethics which they must follow.

Third, the cults give a person a functioning job for support by giving them simple tasks to perform in which they can easily achieve success in. In turn, the cult gives them food, lodging, and support.

Fourth, the philosophy of the cult or the cult leader is overlaid on top of the individual thought process. Instead of building a meaningful philosophy of life for themselves, these individuals become dependent and accept the philosophy given to them by the cult leaders.

The completed recruitment process produces people who will now find their dependence and security within the cult rather than developing their own security and the independence of a mature individual.

Moonie Theology

What exactly is the theology that Moon is teaching these young people? Moon has a very different and interesting theology. In his *Divine Principle* he lays out what he believes to be the true doctrine of man.

Moon says that God created Adam and Eve and that Eve fell into sin through sexual relations with Satan. She passed that sin on to the whole human race. He claims it was then necessary for a second Adam, a new Jesus Christ, to come to earth in order to marry a sinless, perfect, and ideal wife so that they might sexually procreate the Kingdom of God on earth.

He states that Jesus came for the purpose of marrying the ideal wife and creating the perfect family. But he says that somewhere along the line, Jesus got sidetracked from his original goal and mistakenly got himself crucified. Therefore, Moon says, there needed to be a second coming of the Messiah, one who would physically bring in the Kingdom of God. He says this new Messiah was born in Korea in 1920.

This just happens to be the very place and time of Moon's birth. Moon also says the Messiah must come out of the New Israel, which is South Korea.

Moon is heavily involved in anticommunist activities, saying that the Communists are the incarnation of Satan and that South Korea is the battle line between God and Satan. This is one of the reasons he is seeking to gain support for South Korea.

He refers again and again to that supposed visitation in 1936, on a hillside in North Korea, where he was chosen to complete the unfinished task of salvation and to physically redeem the world. That work includes the divine need for him to have sexual relations with 70 virgins, 70 married women, and 70 widows so that he might procreate the Kingdom of God on earth.

With a theology like that, it's no wonder he was excommunicated from the Presbyterian Church in 1948!

Moon now claims that the New Age was ushered in when he married his fourth wife. He says the first three were not pure enough. He now teaches that his fourth wife is the Holy Spirit incarnate, that their marriage in 1960 was the marriage feast of the Lamb recorded in Revelation 19, and that their 11 children are now sinless offspring who are going to sexually bring in the Kingdom of God on earth.

The Warnings from Scripture

The Bible warns us again and again about the coming of such messiahs.

Dear friends, although I was very eager to write to you about the salvation we share, I felt I had to write and urge you to contend for the faith that was once for all entrusted to the saints. For certain men whose condemnation was written about long ago have secretly slipped in among you. They are godless men, who change the grace of our God into a license for immorality and deny Jesus Christ our only Sovereign and Lord (Jude 3,4).

There were also false prophets among the people, just as there will be false teachers among you. They will secretly introduce destructive heresies, even denying the sovereign Lord who bought them—bringing swift destruction on themselves. Many will follow their shameful ways and will bring the way of truth into disrepute. In their greed these teachers will exploit you with stories they have made up. Their condemnation has long been hanging over them, and their destruction has not been sleeping (2 Peter 2:1-3).

This is precisely what we see with Sun Myung Moon. He has denied the Lord Jesus Christ, he is exploiting young people with false words, and he is turning the gospel into his own sexual license. It seems that whenever a person goes away from the worship of the true and living God and goes outside the framework that God has given us in the Bible, he always ends up in this type of perversion.

Moon teaches that he alone is the true parent of mankind, that he alone is the ruler and the authority. His followers must reject their own biological parents and have nothing to do with them. Moon now teaches his followers that they must atone for their sins and the sins of their ancestors through nonstop exhaustion and total servitude to Father Moon.

The Biblical Message

What does the Bible say about such teachings?

> When the kindness and love of God our Savior appeared, he saved us, not because of righteous things we had done, but because of his mercy. He saved us through the washing of rebirth and renewal by the Holy Spirit, whom he poured out on us generously through Jesus Christ our Savior, so that, having been justified by his grace, we might become heirs having the hope of eternal life (Titus 3:4-7).

Paul says in Galatians 2 that if there were any way you could earn your salvation, then Christ died needlessly. Salvation is through *the grace of God*, and grace is something God gives you which you do not deserve. Through faith alone in Jesus Christ we have salvation and redemption.

But Moon, like all the cult leaders, wants to do away with the blood of Jesus Christ. One of the common things we hear from former Moonies is that they were continually told that the death of Jesus Christ was meaningless, that Jesus failed, and that the power of the cross of Jesus is a myth. He instructs his followers that they must hate the blood and cross of Jesus Christ in order to be set free from their influence.

However, the Bible says, "The message of the cross is foolishness to those who are perishing, but to us who are being saved it is the power of God" (1 Corinthians 1:18).

Paul claimed that he was determined to know Jesus Christ and Him crucified. It was Paul who also said:

> May I never boast except in the cross of our Lord Jesus Christ, through which the world has been crucified to me, and I to the world (Galatians 6:14).

The religions of the world are man's attempts to reach God through his good works, through his rituals, through his sacrifices, through his money. But God says this cannot work because man is affected with the spiritual disease called sin.

God, who is holy, cannot look on our sins. Because man

could not reach God, the great truth of Christianity is that *God reached down to man in Jesus Christ.* Through His sacrificially shed blood on Calvary's cross Jesus made a way for us to come back to a relationship with the Father.

Romans 5:8 says, "God demonstrates his own love for us in this: While we were still sinners, Christ died for us."

11

Mormonism: The Church of Jesus Christ of Latter-day Saints

We need to take the very complicated theology of Mormonism and break it down to its simplest elements if we are to help you respond with knowledge and confidence to friends or loved ones caught up in one of today's most seductive non-Christian religions. We want to give you a few of the answers for the tough questions posed by Mormonism.

Mormonism is no longer some quaint, quiet religious sect buried in the creases of the everlasting hills of Utah. Its presence is now felt worldwide. No doubt you have seen the rash of ads for the Mormon Church in *Reader's Digest* and in *TV Guide*.

Coupled with their very effective "family-oriented" public service spots on TV and radio, the Mormons are blitzing the U.S. and Canada with "name familiarity." Few homes in North America have escaped the regular visits of the Mormon missionaries.

A Mormon source recently indicated that between the free PSA TV ads and their paid advertising, including

regional newspaper inserts and national magazine advertising, the Mormons expect to spend over 100 million
dollars in annual advertising costs in the 1990's to get
multiple messages of their faith into every North American
home.

This would be exciting news if that message were one of
true Christian substance, but unfortunately that is not the
case.

Beyond the Facade

In order to understand Mormonism from the historic
Christian perspective, we need to step beyond the highly
professional facade that is presented to us in the LDS ads.

They show us only what the Mormon church wants us to
see: a caring, sensitive church with Christ-centered families, all working together for the furthering of Christ's work
on earth.

Some of this is true! In one sense these are committed,
loving people whose conscious intent is not to be the ene-
mies of Christ. Many Mormons sincerely believe they are
serving Christ and His final message of end-times instruc-
tions.

Most Mormons are victims of a deception as clever as
anything thrown at the world since the days of Adam. But,
tragically, even though they may be victims, they do great
harm to the true cause of Christ.

What is behind the Madison Avenue image? What is
really wrong with Mormonism? Let's look at a few crucial
issues.

In his letter to the Galatians the apostle Paul says:

> I am astonished that you are so quickly deserting
> the one who called you by the grace of Christ and are
> turning to a different gospel—which is really no gos-
> pel at all. Evidently some people are throwing you into
> confusion and are trying to pervert the gospel of
> Christ. But even if we or an angel from heaven should
> preach a gospel other than the one we preached to
> you, let him be eternally condemned! (Galatians 1:6-8).

For "eternally condemned" Paul uses the strongest possible Greek term, *anathema*, which means *under the divine curse*. To emphasize his point, he repeats it again in verse 9:

> As we have already said, so now I say again: If anybody is preaching to you a gospel other than what you accepted, let him be eternally condemned!

Why do we begin our study of Mormonism with that passage? For the simple reason that Mormonism began in the year 1820 with several visitations from alleged messengers from heaven who came to young Joseph Smith Jr. and told him some very interesting things—things that were directly contradictory to the revealed Word of God.

The Law of Eternal Progression

The major heresy of Mormonism is summed up in its central theological axiom, the doctrine of the law of eternal progression. To believe in and teach this doctrine is to be so separated from Christian orthodoxy that the unrepentant adherent is consigned to a Christless eternity. It is stated as follows:

> As man is, God once was,
> and as God is, man may become.

Roll that through your mind a time or two: *"As man is, God once was, and as God is, man may become."*

This all starts with the LDS teaching that there are great numbers of planets scattered throughout the vastness of outer space which are ruled by countless exalted men-gods who once were human like us.

This may all sound like Battlestar Galactica to the average person, but upon this axiom is based the entire theology of Mormonism: from the temple rituals for the living to those for their dead; from the teaching that families are forever to the pressure on parents to send their youth to the mission fields across the world.

The Mormon people are committed to a controlled program that maps out their entire lives as they seek their own exaltation and godhood, their own planet to rule and reign over.

Let's look at this mystery religion in simple terms. Perhaps the most basic work we ever did in this area was to summarize the core Mormon doctrine and put it together in a short animation sequence for the movie *The God Makers*. Let's go through the actual script of that sequence for you.

Mormonism teaches that trillions of planets scattered throughout the cosmos are ruled by countless gods who once were human like us.

They say that long ago on one of these planets, to an unidentified god and one of his goddess wives, a spirit child named Elohim was conceived. This spirit child was later born to human parents who gave him a physical body.

Through obedience to Mormon teaching, death, and resurrection, he proved himself worthy and was elevated to godhood as his father before him.

Mormons believe that Elohim is their heavenly Father and that he lives with his many wives on a planet near a mysterious star called Kolob. Here the god of Mormonism and his wives, through endless celestial sex, produced billions of spirit children.

To decide their destiny, the head of the Mormon gods called a great heavenly council meeting. Both of Elohim's eldest sons were there, Lucifer and his brother Jesus.

A plan was presented to build planet Earth, where the spirit children would be sent to take on mortal bodies and learn good from evil. Lucifer stood and made his bid for becoming savior of this new world. Wanting the glory for himself, he planned to force everyone to become gods. Opposing the idea, the Mormon Jesus suggested giving man his freedom of choice, as on other planets. The vote that followed approved the proposal of the Mormon Jesus, who would become savior of the planet Earth.

Enraged, Lucifer cunningly convinced one-third of the spirits destined for Earth to fight with him and revolt. Thus Lucifer became the devil and his followers the demons. Sent to this world in spirit form, they would forever be denied bodies of flesh and bone.

Those who remained neutral in the battle were cursed to be born with black skin. This is the Mormon explanation for the Negro race. The spirits that fought most valiantly against Lucifer would be born into Mormon families on planet Earth. These would be the lighter-skinned people, or "white and delightsome," as the Book of Mormon described them.

Early Mormon prophets taught that Elohim and one of his goddess wives came to Earth as Adam and Eve to start the human race. Thousands of years later, Elohim in human form once again journeyed to Earth from the star base Kolob, this time to have physical relations with the Virgin Mary in order to provide Jesus with a physical body.

Mormon Apostle Orson Hyde taught that after Jesus Christ grew to manhood he took at least three wives: Mary, Martha, and Mary Magdalene. Through these wives the Mormon Jesus supposedly fathered a number of children before he was crucified. Mormon founder Joseph Smith is supposedly one of his descendants.

According to the Book of Mormon, after his resurrection Jesus came to the Americas to preach to the Indians, who the Mormons believe are really Israelites. Thus the Jesus of Mormonism established his church in the Americas as he had in Palestine. By the year 421 A.D., the dark-skinned Israelites, known as the Lamanites, had destroyed all of the white-skinned Nephites in a number of great battles. The Nephites' records were supposedly written on golden plates buried in the Hill Cumorah by Moroni, the last living Nephite.

About 1400 years later a young treasure-seeker named Joseph Smith, who was known for his tall tales, claimed to have uncovered the same gold plates near his home in upstate New York. He is now honored by Mormons as a prophet because he claimed to have had visions from the spirit world in which he was commanded to organize the Mormon Church because all Christian creeds were an abomination. It was Joseph Smith who originated most of these peculiar doctrines which millions today believe to be true.

By maintaining a rigid code of financial and moral requirements, and through performing secret temple rituals for themselves and the dead, the Latter-day Saints hope to prove their worthiness and thus become gods. The Mormons teach that everyone must stand at the final judgment before Joseph Smith, the Mormon Jesus, and Elohim.

Those Mormons who are sealed in the eternal marriage ceremony in LDS temples expect to become polygamous gods or their goddess wives in the Celestial Kingdom, rule over other planets, and spawn new families throughout eternity. The Mormons thank God for Joseph Smith, who claimed that he had done more for us than any other man, including Jesus Christ. The Mormons claim that he died as a martyr, shedding his blood for us so that we too may become gods.

Shocking? Incomprehensible? Maybe to you and to us, but *this is the core of Mormon theology*. It binds its believers away from the real Jesus, the real gospel, and the real spirit of truth as surely as though they were locked away in chains of metal.

The Mormon Jesus

To the Mormon, Jesus was our elder brother who pointed the way, but he isn't The Way as we Christians understand it.

To the Mormon, Jesus was the god of the Old Testament, but once he took his physical form, he had to justify or earn his own spiritual salvation through his works while in the flesh, just as each of us must.

Mormonism teaches that Jesus suffered for our sins in the Garden of Gethsemane, providing personal salvation (which may mean exaltation to godhood) conditional upon our obedience to the laws and ordinances of the LDS gospel. His death on the cross provided a *general* salvation, whereby all of us will be resurrected to be judged for our own works. Yet Paul says in Colossians 2 that Jesus removed those laws and ordinances that were against us, nailing them to the cross.

It is no wonder that you will never see a cross on a Mormon church—not when you see that Mormons cannot deal with its gift of grace. This is the same reason they use water for communion. They call it The Sacrament, but that water washes away the reality of the blood shed for us at the cross of Christ.

Jesus is the LDS savior only in the sense that his death gives the Mormon the means of returning to the god of this world, using the secret keys, handgrips, and passwords learned only in the Mormon Temple, secrets that will ensure safe passage through the doorway to personal godhood.

What we have shared is just the tip of a dark and dangerous iceberg, filled with death for its unsuspecting victims.

Proverbs 14:12 says:

> There is a way which seems right to a man, but its end is the way of death (NKJV).

Was a Scripture ever more direct in a life-or-death issue? The Mormon people are like those of whom Paul spoke in Romans 10:1-3:

> Brethren, my heart's desire and prayer to God . . . is that they may be saved. For I bear them witness that they have a zeal for God, but not according to knowledge. For they being ignorant of God's righteousness, and seeking to establish their own righteousness, have not submitted to the righteousness of God (NKJV).

The Mormon God

Mormons teach four basic points on the doctrine of God. First, Mormons teach that God the Father has a body of flesh and bone as tangible as man's.

Second, Mormons teach that God evolved from mortal man. Mormons believe that God is a finite man who has been evolving and changing to become God and now is a man-God in heaven with a body of flesh and bone, an exalted man who is God over this planet.

Third, Mormons teach polytheism. Polytheism is the belief in the existence of more than one god. Mormons believe there are literally millions of gods: father gods, mother gods, grandfather gods, grandmother gods, great-grandfather gods, great-grandmother gods, aunts and uncles—literally millions of gods.

Fourth, every male Mormon is striving to become a god himself. Let's see what the first two Mormon prophets, Joseph Smith and Brigham Young, said about the doctrine of God.

We quote a sermon given by Joseph Smith Jr. two months before he was killed in Carthage, Illinois, in 1844. This sermon was heard by over 18,000 people. It was taken down by five Mormon scribes and published in the official Mormon publication *Times and Seasons*, volume 5, page 613.

It is also found in the LDS encyclopedic work *Mormon Doctrine* by Bruce R. McConkie, page 321.

> God was once as we are now, an exalted man, and sits enthroned in yonder heavens. I say if you were to see him today you would see him like a man in form like yourselves and all the person and image of man. I am going to tell you how God came to be God. We have imagined that God was God from all eternity. I will refute that idea and take away the veil. God was once a man like us and dwelt on an earth, the same as Jesus Christ did, and you have got to learn to be gods yourselves the same as all gods before you. Namely by going from one small degree to another, from a small capacity to a greater one.

Brigham Young goes on to say:

> The Lord created you and me for the purpose of becoming gods like himself. We are created to become gods like unto our father in heaven (*Journal of Discourses*, volume 10, page 223). Gods exist and we had better strive to become one with them. . . . A plurality of gods exist, indeed this doctrine of plurality of gods is so comprehensive and glorious that it reaches out and embraces every exalted personage. Those who attain exaltation are gods (*Mormon Doctrine*, page 577).

This concept isn't something taught a century ago but is no longer considered doctrine. The *Church News* is the official weekly news publication of the LDS Church. On September 9, 1989, appeared an interesting article about the nature of God.

> The prophet Joseph Smith also made significant contribution to the world's limited understanding of the godhead. Perhaps one doctrine that most distinguishes Latter-day Saints from other denominations is the conviction that all worthy men and women can become gods and goddesses.

Journal of Discourses, volume 1, page 121, says this:

> Remember that God our heavenly Father was once a child and mortal like we are, and rose step by step in the scale of progress, and in the school of advancement has moved forward and overcome until he has arrived at the point where he is now.

Doctrine and Covenants, one of the standard works of the Mormon faith, states in Section 130, verse 22:

> God the Father has a body of flesh and bone as tangible as man's.

This is actual Mormon doctrine and theology. We must test it against the teaching of God's Word.

To begin with, Mormons teach that God the Father has a body of flesh and bone as tangible as man's. What does the Bible say about this?

In the Gospel of John chapter 4 we have a New Testament statement concerning the nature of the Father. It is given to us by Jesus Christ Himself, the One who knows better than anybody else. Jesus said:

> You Samaritans worship what you do not know; we worship what we do know, for salvation is from the Jews. Yet a time is coming and has now come when the true worshipers will worship the Father in spirit and

truth, for they are the kind of worshipers the Father seeks. God is spirit, and his worshipers must worship in spirit and in truth (John 4:22-24).

Jesus said, "God is spirit." The logical question to ask is: What is a spirit? In Luke 24 Jesus defined what a spirit is. After His resurrection He appeared to the two disciples on the road to Emmaus and then His other disciples. They were startled and frightened and thought they were seeing a spirit.

They were startled and frightened, thinking they saw a ghost [spirit]. He said to them, "Why are you troubled, and why do doubts rise in your minds? Look at my hands and my feet. It is I myself! Touch me and see; a ghost does not have flesh and bones, as you see I have." When he had said this, he showed them his hands and feet (Luke 24:37-40).

Several years before he died, one of the very elderly apostles of the Mormon Church, Le Grand Richards, was presenting an apologetic trying to prove that God was a man in heaven with a body of flesh and bone. (This was during the Mormon semiannual conference being broadcast from Salt Lake City.)

He had just finished trying to prove his point when he went on to talk about who Jesus Christ was. The first verse he read was Matthew 16:13, but as he kept reading over national television his voice gradually tapered off to silence when he became aware that he should not be reading verse 17 after what he had just finished trying to prove!

In verse 13 Jesus asked His disciples, "Who do men say that I am?" Simeon Peter answered:

"You are the Christ, the Son of the living God." Jesus answered and said to him, "Blessed are you Simeon Bar-Jonah, for flesh and blood has not revealed this to you, but My Father who is in heaven" (Matthew 16:16,17 NKJV).

Jesus clearly taught that the LDS doctrine of God having a body of flesh and blood is false. Jesus said that God is spirit, and that a spirit does not have flesh and bone, nor a body of flesh and blood.

Mormons teach that God evolved from mortal man. When the Mormon Tabernacle Choir sings the anthems of the Church, they are not singing about the God of the Bible. They are singing about a finite man of flesh and bone who has been evolving and changing to become a god. Is God a finite man who has been evolving and changing, as the Mormons claim? What does God's Word say?

In Numbers 23:19 we read, "God is not a man, that he should lie, nor a son of man, that he should change his mind."

In Hosea 11:9 we read, "I am God, and not man—the Holy One among you."

God is not a man who has been evolving and changing. In Malachi 3:6 we read, "I the Lord do not change."

In Psalm 90:2 we read, "From everlasting to everlasting you are God."

God is not in the process of evolving and changing. The Bible says that from everlasting to everlasting, God is God.

What the Mormons have ended up worshiping is a finite man of flesh and bone who is evolving and changing. But this is not the eternal, infinite, immutable God of the Bible! The Bible tells us what God thinks of the Mormon deity in Romans chapter 1.

> Although they claimed to be wise, they became fools and exchanged the glory of the immortal God for images made to look like mortal man. . . . They exchanged the truth of God for a lie (Romans 1:22,23,25).

This is precisely what the Mormons have done.

The Mormons also teach polytheism—the belief in the existence of more than one God. They teach that there are literally millions of gods in the Mormon pantheon. What does the Bible say about this? Here are some good verses to share with the next Mormon missionary who comes to your door.

This is what the Lord says—Israel's King and Redeemer, the Lord Almighty: "I am the first and I am
the last; apart from me there is no God" (Isaiah 44:6).

Is there any God besides me? No, there is no other
Rock; I know not one (Isaiah 44:8).

If God Himself doesn't know of any other gods, how
could the Mormons know of millions of gods?

I am the Lord, and there is no other; apart from me
there is no God (Isaiah 45:5).

Surely God is with you, and there is no other; there
is no other god (Isaiah 45:14).

There is no God apart from me, a righteous God
and a Savior; there is none but me (Isaiah 45:21).

Turn to me and be saved, all you ends of the earth;
for I am God, and there is no other (Isaiah 45:22).

Do you see the pattern of what God says?

To whom will you compare me or count me equal?
To whom will you liken me that we may be compared?
(Isaiah 46:5).

Remember the former things, those of long ago; I
am God, and there is no other; I am God, and there is
none like me! (Isaiah 46:9).

God says that there isn't anyone like Him! He is the first
and He is the last, and besides Him there is no other god!
Simply put, the difference between Mormonism and Christianity is the difference between polytheism and monotheism. Nowhere in the history of the church or Scripture
could a polytheist ever be a follower of God. In fact it was
for polytheism that God destroyed the nations around
Israel, and it was for polytheism that God destroyed Israel
and sent it into exile in 722 B.C. It was for polytheism that
God destroyed Judah in 586 B.C. and sent it into exile. *God
absolutely condemns polytheism.*

Yet part of the Mormon doctrine of God is the belief that every male Mormon can become a god himself! Joseph Smith said, "You have got to learn to become gods yourselves the same as all gods before you." Brigham Young said, "The Lord created you and me for the purpose of becoming gods like himself. We are created to become gods like unto our father in heaven."

Is it possible to become gods? What does God say in His Word?

> "You are my witnesses," declares the Lord, "and my servant whom I have chosen, so that you may know and believe me and understand that I am he. Before me no god was formed, nor will there be one after me" (Isaiah 43:10).

Joseph Smith

We do not have space to go into all the background of Joseph Smith Jr. He was known in the region of New York near Palmyra for digging for buried treasure and using occult seer stones to divine for hidden treasure. In fact, Michael Quinn, onetime Professor of History at Brigham Young University, wrote a book entitled *Early Mormonism in the Magic World View*.

It clearly documents the fact that Joseph Smith was heavily involved in the occult before he ever began to receive revelations from his messengers of light. Mr. Quinn is no longer with BYU or the LDS church. While the LDS cannot refute his scholarship, they have nevertheless repudiated him personally.

Joseph Smith claimed that he went into the woods near his home to pray and inquire of God which of all the Christian churches was right and which one he should join.

He recorded this event for us in his own words, and that story is now considered Scripture by the LDS church and sits as part of the standard works of the Mormon Church, in what is called *The Pearl of Great Price*. We find this quote in the book Joseph Smith, chapter 2, verses 15-19.

I knelt down and began to offer up the desire of my heart to God. I had scarcely done so when immediately I was seized upon by some power which entirely overcame me and had such an astonishing influence over me as to bind my tongue so that I could not speak.

Thick darkness gathered around me and it seemed to me for a time as if I were doomed to sudden destruction. But exerting all my powers to call upon God to deliver me out of the power of this enemy which had seized upon me and at the very moment when I was ready to sink into despair and abandon myself to destruction—not to an imaginary ruin, but to the power of some actual being from the unseen world, who had such marvelous powers as I never before felt in any being—just at this moment of great alarm, I saw a pillar of light exactly over my head, above the brightness of the sun, which descended gradually until it fell upon me. It no sooner appeared than I found myself delivered from the enemy which held me bound. When the light rested upon me I saw two Personages, whose brightness and glory defy all descriptions, standing above me in the air. One of them spake unto me, calling me by name and said pointing to the other—"this is my beloved son, hear him."

My object in going to inquire of the Lord was to know which of all the [Christian churches or] sects was right that I might know which to join. No sooner, therefore, did I get possession of myself so as to be able to speak, than I asked the Personages who stood above me in the light which of all the sects [the Christian churches] was right and which I should join.

We want you to get the picture of what is happening here. Joseph Smith, already involved in the occult, said he went out into the woods to pray and that he was seized upon by some powerful being of the unseen world.

He said thick darkness gathered around him. His tongue was held bound so that he could not speak and he was sinking into despair, ready to succumb to this *actual being from the unseen world who had such marvelous powers*, when all of a sudden there appeared over his head a pillar of light in which were two personages.

He asked these personages, these beings of light, which Christian church was right and which one should he join. Here is what he claims they answered (verse 19).

> I was answered that I must join none of them, for they were all wrong; and the Personage who addressed me said that all of their creeds were an abomination in his sight, and that all their teachers were corrupt.

This moment in 1820 was the moment that opened the door to Mormonism. A messenger of light told Joseph Smith that all the Christian churches were wrong and that all the teachings of Christianity were an abomination.

That means this personage of light was telling Joseph Smith that the trinity, the deity of Jesus Christ, the blood atonement of Calvary, and salvation by faith in Jesus Christ were all an abomination!

We need to ask ourselves, "Who was this personage of light in 1820 telling Joseph Smith that all the teachings of Christianity were an abomination? Who was speaking from that pillar of light?"

Where did this different gospel come from? The apostle Paul answers the question for us:

> I am jealous for you with a godly jealousy. I promised you to one husband, to Christ, so that I might present you as a pure virgin to him. But I am afraid that just as Eve was deceived by the serpent's cunning, your minds may somehow be led astray from your sincere and pure devotion to Christ. For if someone comes to you and preaches a Jesus other than the Jesus we preached, or if you receive a different spirit from the one you received, or a different gospel from the one you accepted, you put up with it easily enough.
>
> For such men are false apostles, deceitful workmen, masquerading as apostles of Christ. And no wonder, for Satan himself masquerades as an angel of light. It is not surprising, then, if his servants masquerade as

servants of righteousness. Their end will be what their actions deserve (2 Corinthians 11:2-5,13-15).

Was Joseph a Prophet?

What about the Mormon Church's claim of a latter-day prophet? Was Joseph Smith a true prophet of God?

The Mormon missionaries ask their prospects to pray and ask God to reveal to them, through a burning in the bosom, whether Joseph Smith was a true prophet.

Many people have prayed that prayer and received that burning in the bosom. Others have had visits from the spirits of their dead ancestors, telling them that the Mormon Church is true and that Smith was a true prophet.

People sometimes wonder why this happens when the inquirer was so sincere. How could God not answer correctly? The problem is that *it wasn't God who answered!* The reason for this is that *the question comes through false teachers.* The Bible states:

> The Lord is near to all who call on him, to all who call on him in truth (Psalm 145:18).

The key words are *"all who call on him in truth."* Submitted to false teachers, these people are victims being led to a spiritual slaughter. They are not calling upon God in truth. In biblical truth, we do not pray about a prophet being true or false; we *test him according to the written Word of God.*

The first clue that something is wrong with the LDS prophet is the fact that the missionaries are *unable* (not always unwilling) to give you a list of the prophecies of Joseph Smith (or of any of their other prophets, for that matter).

At the time of this writing, in early 1994, the present prophet, Ezra Taft Benson, is extremely elderly and has difficulty recognizing family members or those who feed him. (His grandson was just censured by the church for stating that fact publicly, and he left the Mormon Church over it.)

The LDS Church has never produced an official list of Smith's prophecies, even though the Church is being led by a living prophet and these prophecies are the single most important aspect of the "restored gospel."

Why? Is it because the Church is unable to compile one? Hardly! There is a different reason: Of the 65 to 70 prophecies that were recorded, only five or six actually came to pass! That's a pretty poor record even for the worst of prophets. The Bible states:

> A prophet who presumes to speak in my name anything I have not commanded him to say, or a prophet who speaks in the name of other gods, must be put to death. You may say to yourselves, "How can we know when a message has not been spoken by the Lord?" If what a prophet proclaims in the name of the Lord does not take place or come true, that is a message the Lord has not spoken. That prophet has spoken presumptuously. Do not be afraid of him (Deuteronomy 18:20-22).

Let's go back to the real heart of the heresy—what Joseph Smith said about the nature of God. Is God a man? The Bible says He is not a man that He should lie. Jesus said that God is *spirit* rather than flesh and bone. The statements of Scripture should settle the issue on the nature of God.

The Bible says in Hebrews chapter 1 that in times *past* God spoke through holy men and prophets but that today He speaks to us by His Son!

Who Will You Trust?

Who are you going to trust for your salvation, man or God? In trusting God, *fully* trust Him for your salvation. Trust in that sin offering of Christ offered up once for all.

There is a zeal to serve God seen in the actions of the Mormon people, but it is a terribly misguided zeal. We pray that you will have the opportunity to share that true joy of Christ's righteousness and love with your Mormon friends and loved ones!

Let them know that there is only one God, who is infinite and eternal, and is not a man. There is only one Savior, Jesus Christ, who took all the laws and ordinances that were against us and moved them out of the way, nailing them to His cross (Colossians 2:13-15).

A man is not justified by observing the law, but by faith in Jesus Christ. So we too have put our faith in Christ Jesus that we may be justified by faith in Christ and not by observing the law, because by observing the law no one will be justified (Galatians 2:16).

12

The New Age Movement

So much has been said and written lately about the New Age movement that you almost need a directory to sort out all the material. A recent article in one of the national magazines said that books and articles dealing with the New Age accounted for approximately half of all Christian bookstore sales in the early 1990's!

What is the New Age? That is the first question everyone asks. A precise definition is difficult to pull together even from the scores of books and articles on the subject. However, the beginnings of the movement are as old as sin itself.

> The serpent was more crafty than any of the wild animals the Lord God had made. He said to the woman, "Did God really say, 'You must not eat from any tree in the garden'?" The woman said to the serpent, "We may eat fruit from the trees in the garden, but God did say, 'You must not eat fruit from the tree that is in the middle of the garden, and you must not touch it, or you will die.'" "You will not surely die," the serpent said to the woman. "For God knows that when you eat of it your eyes will be opened, and you will be like God, knowing good and evil." When the woman saw that the fruit of the tree was good for food and pleasing to the eye, and also desirable for gaining wisdom, she took some and ate it. She also gave some

to her husband, who was with her, and he ate it (Genesis 3:1-6).

Like the promise of the serpent, the New Age teaches that:

1. God's Word cannot be trusted entirely (verses 1,4,5).

2. Man does not have to die (verse 4).

3. Man can become a god (verse 5).

4. Man can evolve through hidden knowledge (verse 6).

New Age Definitions

The New Age has its own definitions of spiritual issues:

1. GOD: No personal God at all; just a cosmic force, a fragment of which is in us; therefore we are gods. There is often a male/female polarity in this "force" (yin-yang).

2. JESUS: A man who evolved into an Ascended Master (godlike being) through occult and metaphysical disciplines.

3. CHRIST: An impersonal "force" which rested on the man Jesus and made him special, but which has also rested on others, and can even rest on us.

4. THE BIBLE: At best a work of cabalistic secrets which can only be understood by "Masters." At worst a stupid book of Jewish legends.

5. SALVATION: By works of occult discipline. The law of karma is irresistible and is what judges us.

6. DENIAL OF DEATH: Belief in reincarnation. Most New Agers believe that humans can evolve into gods through many lifetimes.

7. MAGICAL WORLDVIEW: View of universe as a machine that can be manipulated through sophisticated mental and spiritual technology—no sovereign God.

8. INTOLERANCE OF MONOTHEISM: Jews, Christians, and Muslims regarded as counterrevolutionary. They must either evolve or be purified.

Roots of the New Age

Historical antecedents of the New Age movement can be found in several major religious groups:

1. Witchcraft and shamanism (prehistoric)
2. Astrology (c. 2000 B.C.)
3. Hinduism and Yoga (c. 1800 B.C.)

The recent doctrinal ancestors of the New Age movement can be found within the dogma of several nineteenth-century cults:

1. *Swedenborgianism (c. 1792)*
   a) Communication with the dead
   b) Spiritual evolution
   c) Denial of the Trinity

2. *Mormonism (c. 1830)*
   a) Man can become a god
   b) Preexistence
   c) Salvation through secret knowledge
   d) Confusion between matter and spirit

3. *Spiritualism (1848)*
   a) Belief in communication with the dead
   b) Cultivation of mediumistic powers (channeling)
   c) Reincarnation

4. *Christian Science and the Mind Science cults (c. 1862)*
   a) God is a force, not a person
   b) Mind can control matter; reality is what you make it
   c) Sin does not exist, nor does death

5. *The Theosophical Society and Lucis Trust (1875)*
   a) Christianity regarded as de-evolutionary
   b) Belief in Ascended Masters who guide the earth
   c) "Root races" and an evolutionary "Plan" for mankind
   d) "Spiritual racism" and anti-Semitism

Ferment of the Sixties and Seventies

The immediate beginnings of the New Age movement can be found in the cultural ferment of the 1960's:

1. The hippie counterculture

2. Interest in drugs and mysticism

3. Destruction of traditional morality

4. Feminism, Wicca, and ecology

5. Humanistic and transpersonal psychology

6. World disarmament and various "hunger" projects

7. Secular humanism

In the early 1970's, Alvin Toffler wrote a book titled *Future Shock*. In it he showed that we were being bombarded with all the elements of massive future shock. Something radical was happening to our society. Toffler said that the pace of change was picking up at such a rate that the curve was going off the chart.

Toffler talked about a soldier in battle being bombarded from every side with bullets, screams, groans, explosions, shells bursting, rapid machine-gun fire, flares lighting up the sky, etc. In such an overstimulating environment a soldier is sometimes pushed beyond his limits, "beyond the upper reaches of his adaptive range." Army doctors call it "long-range penetration strain."

A form of this problem has permeated every sector of our society. Its symptoms are mental deterioration, fatigue, emotional exhaustion. Its victims become dull and listless, irrational, confused, mindless, dazed, and bewildered.

We have become a nation and a world of confused people running in the wrong direction. To the many people without an anchor, without a standard by which to direct their lives, the world has become a surrealistic nightmare. They collectively end up with a subjective feeling of loss and a sense of isolation and loneliness caused by this massive bombardment of the senses. This phenomenon has a purpose and goal orchestrated by the master of deceit himself:

He wants us to believe that relief lies in the teachings of the New Age.

Worldwide Phenomenon

All of this is not simply a phenomenon in the United States, but is sweeping around the world and becoming the predominant philosophy around the world.

The number-one television program in Russia today features a New Age psychic and channeler who is on every morning in Moscow. His program has captivated the nation.

As Ron recently traveled on a speaking tour abroad, he saw that in Great Britain and throughout the European continent, the New Age movement is becoming the predominant philosophy of the 1990's.

When Ron was in New Delhi he saw an article in the *Delhi Times* stating that the New Age movement has created a revival of Hindu nationalism because Americans are finally accepting Hinduism as a true religion.

Billy Graham spoke to a large conference on evangelism in Amsterdam several years ago. In that message he pointed out the well-known fact that inside the heart of every man and woman in the world is a large, empty hole that can only be filled with the holiness of God. God designed us with that hole filled with His presence in the Garden of Eden, but when we separated ourselves from Him, our spiritual systems became defective.

The only thing that will ever fill our emptiness is God Himself. Until man steps back into fellowship with God through Jesus Christ, that emptiness will just continue to cause us to ache. All too many people have tried to fill that emptiness with everything except the Lord, and this holds especially true for those people lost in the lies of the New Age.

The apostle Paul said:

> The message of the cross is foolishness to those who are perishing, but to us who are being saved it is the power of God. For it is written: "I will destroy the

wisdom of the wise; the intelligence of the intelligent I will frustrate." Where is the wise man? Where is the scholar? Where is the philosopher of this age? Has not God made foolish the wisdom of the world? For since in the wisdom of God the world through its wisdom did not know him, God was pleased through the foolishness of what was preached to save those who believe. Jews demand miraculous signs and Greeks look for wisdom (1 Corinthians 1:18-22).

Notice specifically verse 21, where Paul said that the world through its wisdom has not come to know God. We are seeing more of the wisdom of the world embracing the New Age movement. Despite the reality of the true and living God all about them, many people are blinded by the same deceiver who promised godhood to our first parents in the Garden of Eden. It is as if a whole section of society is running blindly in the streets. But the Word of God says:

The god of this age has blinded the minds of unbelievers, so that they cannot see the light of the gospel of the glory of Christ, who is the image of God (2 Corinthians 4:4).

All the Elements

The New Age came into its own in the 1980's through a number of events which brought together all the elements that comprise the general body of the New Age movement. We need to point out again that there is no single organization and no single leader at whose feet we can lay our charges against the movement; it is a very broad philosophical and religious movement. Some of the contributing elements include:

1. 1980—Marilyn Ferguson writes *The Aquarian Conspiracy*.

2. 1982—The "Coming of Christ" advertising campaign appears in major newspapers with Benjamin Creme's arrival on the scene as Maitreya's "John the Baptist."

3. 1983—Shirley MacLaine emerges as a major media spokesperson for the New Age movement with her book *Out on a Limb*.

4. 1986—Channelers like J.Z. Knight and Lazaris become celebrities.

In the 1980's, the New Age movement became enmeshed in every area of society:

1. Public education has become heavily New Age influenced.

2. Corporations use its techniques for executive training.

3. Political and military leaders push it.

4. The United Nations becomes a major center for promoting it.

5. Many churches teach New Age concepts.

There are two major schools of New Age thought. The first is what we might call Consciousness Renaissance, a permutation in which mankind is stepping beyond its self-imposed limits to merge with the unlimited powers of an already-utopian universe.

This philosophy works from the perspective that man's true mind has been veiled by his own ignorance and limits, and that man is divine and perfect, the world is divine and perfect, the whole cosmos is divine and perfect, and we are all part of the same divinity. We will achieve this state of perfection by unitedly meditating and willing the thing to happen. The more adherents who work at this, the quicker this state of perfection will be reached. All we need to do in order to claim our godhood, both as individuals and as an entire world, is to step into the reality of our perfection and divinity, thereby releasing our god-nature and merging with our own heaven on earth.

The second major branch of New Age thought can be termed the "Quantum Leap of Consciousness." When sufficient momentum is generated by enough people having developed higher consciousness, then the *entire world* will be ready to take that quantum leap into a higher dimension. In contrast to Consciousness Renaissance, this explosion into the New Age will come as we ready ourselves to accept the gift of new life from powers beyond us. This giant step into cosmic reality will take place in a moment of time. It sees mankind on the edge of a massive evolutionary explosion in which we all wake up one morning in a new world where we are all one with divinity and power and goodness.

There are varied concepts as to what form this divine intervention will take: highly evolved humanoids, or some high council of god-men who are the Ascended Masters of another time or another world, or some other all-powerful divine beings who have benevolent motives which are pure, beyond our understanding.

There is a lot of overlapping between the two schools of thought, but the most dangerous school from the Christian perspective is surely the Quantum Leap of Consciousness group. This is because Consciousness Renaissance involves lifting oneself up into godhood, into that utopian heaven that awaits just beyond the third dimension, while Quantum Leap of Consciousness involves mankind interacting with powerful, enlightened entities from outside the human experience.

This second philosophy is much more bent toward the mystical and the occult, with doors open wide to every imaginable demonic force. Every form of witchcraft and black magic is spun into the fabric of this aspect of the New Age.

Vehicle for Judgment

That's where we come in as Christians. The New Age marketeers want us to see the peace and serenity of their movement as an escape from the pressures on a volatile world, when in reality it is the very vehicle by which the world is spiraling downward in its final race toward judgment.

This should come as no surprise to those Christians who have a biblical perspective of human events. The Scripture reminds us:

> The time will come when they will not endure sound doctrine, but according to their own desires, because they have itching ears, they will heap up for themselves teachers; and they will turn their ears away from the truth, and be turned aside to fables (2 Timothy 4:3,4 NKJV).

For all the self-acclaimed wisdom of the proponents of the New Age, they are prime examples of a people who have turned the omnipotent God of the universe into whatever form they wished.

> For although they knew God, they neither glorified him as God nor gave thanks to him, but their thinking became futile and their foolish hearts were darkened. Although they claimed to be wise, they became fools and exchanged the glory of the immortal God for images made to look like mortal man and birds and animals and reptiles. Therefore God gave them over in the sinful desires of their hearts to sexual impurity for the degrading of their bodies with one another. They exchanged the truth of God for a lie, and worshiped and served created things rather than the Creator—who is forever praised. Amen.
>
> Because of this, God gave them over to shameful lusts. Even their women exchanged natural relations for unnatural ones. In the same way the men also abandoned natural relations with women and were inflamed with lust for one another. Men committed indecent acts with other men, and received in themselves the due penalty for their perversion. Furthermore, since they did not think it worthwhile to retain the knowledge of God, he gave them over to a depraved mind, to do what ought not to be done. They have become filled with every kind of wickedness, evil, greed and depravity. They are full of envy, murder, strife, deceit and malice. They are gossips, slanderers, God-haters, insolent, arrogant and boastful; they invent ways of doing evil; they disobey their parents;

they are senseless, faithless, heartless, ruthless. Although they know God's righteous decree that those who do such things deserve death, they not only continue to do these very things but also approve of those who practice them (Romans 1:21-32).

We see New Agers marching for the rights of fur-bearing animals, fish, certain mammals, and even Mother Earth. Should we wonder that their ranks are filled with people given over to the gay and lesbian lifestyles? Even those who abstain from such actual practices support and promote this lifestyle as normal.

In our school systems, children are being exposed to these very things. New-Age-oriented classes, acceptance programs, and school assemblies are going on throughout the country. School hallways and locker areas commonly display posters with phone numbers of gay and lesbian groups for interested students to call. Children all the way down to first grade are being taught to lie on the floor and practice visualization, guided imagery, Yoga, and meditation. They are being told to "go within" and tap into their own divine energy.

Movie stars now openly proclaim their perversions and support the New Age movement both personally and in their art. In 1975, *Time* magazine estimated that there were thousands of Hindu gurus in the United States. This is when we had the introduction of Eastern Hindu mysticism into the recipe; the Eastern cults began to rush into the spiritual vacuum. In 1975, Maharishi Mahesh Yogi, founder of Transcendental Meditation, was on the Merv Griffin Show sitting in his lotus position. Clint Eastwood came walking out on stage with a bouquet of flowers and bowed at the feet of Maharishi.

Then out walked Burt Reynolds with flowers and he too bowed at the feet of Maharishi. Then out walked Mary Tyler Moore and she too bowed at the feet of Maharishi. All three claimed to find peace and fulfillment through transcendental Hindu meditation. To their many millions of fans and admirers, this was as a revelation from the gods.

The Phony Answer

The sweet taste of the "inner peace" of the New Age movement seems to hold the answer to all our problems, and the movement is sweeping the world. *Time* magazine of December 7, 1987, published a major article on Shirley MacLaine promoting the New Age. She had a five-hour miniseries on ABC television entitled "Out on a Limb," based upon her bestselling book by the same title.

According to her story, MacLaine's spiritual search did not lead her to Jesus Christ and the Bible, but to New Age channelers, mediums, and spiritists who told her to go down to the Bolivian Andes in South America, where she was to encounter UFO's that would land and where aliens would communicate the New Age wisdom. When Shirley was asked what this New Age wisdom was, she responded by saying that—

> . . . the New Age is man being divine, man can become God. Man does not need a savior, he can save himself through cyclic rebirth and reincarnation.

Many of the environmental and ecology movements are enthusiastically adopting the New Age movement, for in the New Age the earth is our mother. In order to save ourselves, we need to save Mother Earth because we have all evolved out of the earth. We share the same hydrogen explosion that formed the earth. We are one with it.

This pantheistic worldview actually comes out of Hinduism and Buddhism. From Eastern Hindu mysticism comes the belief in transmigration, known in the West as reincarnation—the doctrine that man can purge himself of sin and karma through cyclic rebirth or reincarnation.

The New Age masters have realized that they can take advantage of the present chaotic state of mankind by offering our disturbed world a tasty kind of peace that soothes the jangled nerves of society without society having to deal with its Creator.

But the solid rock of Calvary has always offered the firm foundation of faith to withstand all the fiery barbs of the onslaught. It holds the answers to all the puzzles and pressures of life and brings an everlasting peace within to everyone who will let go of self and hold on to Christ.

When people refuse to reach out to Calvary and instead try to pull from within themselves, they trade a host of painful, unsolvable problems for a temporary fix known as the New Age movement.

The only way anyone will ever have a true relationship with the mighty, creative God of this universe is through His only begotten Son, Jesus Christ.

13

Fast Facts on

Prosperity Theology: The New Idolatry

The thrust of this book is to prepare you to deal with the spiritual darkness and counterfeits looming today, the false Christs and the false prophets who seek to lead many people astray, even the very elect of the Lord.

But there is also an issue we need to deal with that is not outside the church. Instead, it is a growing heresy that is creeping into the church throughout America. It may even be touching some of your lives right now.

This heresy has come to be known as "prosperity theology." It is being taught by many people on television. It is the teaching that God always wants you healthy, wealthy, and prosperous—that the goal of the Christian life is financial prosperity and health, and if you are not healthy and prosperous, then you are a sinner or you lack faith or you haven't claimed these things by using the right formulas, the correct powers of the tongue.

Recently Ron received a letter in the mail accompanying a package of olive oil. The label of the olive oil read "Holy Bible-anointed oil." The letter said:

> Use this Holy Bible-anointed oil. James 5:14 says to turn God's healing and prosperity on in your life. Are you sick in your body? Use this Holy Bible-anointed oil. Are you sick financially? Use this Holy Bible-anointed oil. Open this Holy Bible-anointed oil. Do not waste a drop.

Jesus is represented by this faith oil. Make a cross on your forehead with it, and then by faith go into your room by yourself and take the money out of your wallet and make a cross on each bill, so that God will heal your money problems. Take your checkbook. Anoint it with this Holy Bible-anointed oil. Then write the largest check you can and anoint it with this Holy Bible-anointed oil and send it to me. I need your support.

This is important to you. When you anoint your money with this Holy Bible-anointed oil, make a cross on each bill and send it to me and God will bless you. Don't waste a drop.

—A man of God for 50 years

Idolatry is not simply worshiping a stone image; idolatry is any concept of God that reduces Him to less than who He really is. There is a false religion growing in our land, and it is called "prosperity theology."

Many Christians are being swept into this false religion by promises of financial prosperity, by claims that God always wants them healthy, wealthy, and prosperous. This "gospel message" has become idolatry by reducing God to someone who is there to give us what we want. This gospel says, "Ask not what you can do for God, but what He can do for you."

American Materialism

This message is a uniquely American charismatic humanism whose emphasis is on man's desire for wealth and his power to direct the actions of God. It is the idolizing of the American value system of success, financial prosperity, and devotion to the here-and-now. It takes secular values and overlays them on Christian teachings, claiming that the real Christians will be at the top of the worldly system, because that's where they deserve to be.

Never mind that our Lord left a secular estate of one torn garment, that He asked one of His disciples to take care of His mother, that He owned no property, that He had no house, that He had no second pair of sandals. Truly His kingdom was not of this world, but was in the heavens. Our King said:

> Do not store up for yourselves treasures on earth, where moth and rust destroy, and where thieves break in and steal. But store up for yourselves treasures in heaven, where moth and rust do not destroy, and where thieves do not break in and steal. For where your treasure is, there your heart will be also (Matthew 6:19-21).

Yet preachers who claim to be following the Carpenter from Nazareth, who didn't even have a permanent place to lay His head, offer vast material riches if viewers will only support their cause. Sometimes the challenge is so blatant as to say, "If you call our toll-free number right now and pledge what God lays on your heart, you can expect great financial blessings this very week." Usually this is followed by someone's testimony who says, "I was sick, I was broke, I was a business failure, and then I gave my life to Jesus. Now I am healthy, wealthy, and a great success."

It all sounds so wonderful: Be a Christian and get a bigger home, a boat, and a vacation in Hawaii. For all too many people, prosperity is becoming the goal of applied Christianity and the mark of true spirituality.

It is no longer, "You shall know them by their love," but "You shall know them by their material possessions." This teaching is creating a generation of Christians who believe that God and all His universe revolve around their own personal comfort and well-being. But it isn't true.

Someone once said that for every hundred people who can successfully handle poverty, there is only one who can successfully handle prosperity. The reason for this is that prosperity comes with its own set of problems.

If the prosperity message were truly God's way, it would put most Christians behind the Iron Curtain and in Third World countries in a pretty bad light, for their testimonies often go something like this: "I had everything: prestige, recognition, a good job, a happy wife, and happy children.

Then I gave my life to Jesus Christ. Now I am in a concentration camp. I've lost my family, my wealth, my reputation, and my health. My crime was that I said I loved Jesus Christ."

Sacrifice in Shanghai

While Ron was recently in Shanghai he spent a Sunday afternoon with a family whose son was an exchange student staying in California. The family were Christians, and the student had asked Ron if he could bring a Bible to his mother and father, since they had not owned a Bible for 20 years. Ron found his way in that city of 10 million people to their apartment building and walked up four flights of broken wooden stairs to a small one-room flat where the father and mother lived.

The father was a brilliant man who has a Ph.D. in nuclear physics. He had been a professor of physics at the University of Shanghai until the Cultural Revolution. The Red Guard came in and burned his books, took the family Bibles, and dismissed him from the university. They told him all he had to do was renounce Jesus Christ in order to get his position back at the university, but he refused. So for the past 20 years he has been relegated to draftsman duties. His wife, a Ph.D. professor of music, has been working as a seamstress for 20 years.

Ron gave these Christians two Bibles, and he will never forget the tears in their eyes as they wept and clutched them to their hearts.

"Let us show you what we have had for spiritual food the last 20 years," the father said. "When the Red Guard came in during the Cultural Revolution, they took all our Bibles and burned them. We were only able to save one old, tattered, beat-up English hymnal." He went to their cedar chest and pulled out the hymnal. "Ron, every night before we go to bed, my wife and I open this hymnal and read a hymn. That has been our only spiritual food for the past 20 years."

Ron asked if they would share some of their favorite hymns. The father turned several pages and began to read,

"I have surrendered all, all to Him I owe." He turned a few more pages and read, "I have decided to follow Jesus; no turning back, no turning back. The world behind me, the cross before me, no turning back, no turning back."

Reality in Laos

A few years ago, Ron was visiting the Cambodian border in Thailand, where there were several hundred thousand Buddhist refugees from Cambodia and Laos. In those camps, you will find no Buddhists taking care of the refugees. There are no Hindus, no Muslims, no Communists providing care.

The ones who were taking care of the refugees were Christians from Christian missions and relief organizations who understand the value of human life.

Ron met a man there who had been a pastor in Laos. Seven years before, the Communists had closed down the radio station in the capital of Laos at which he worked, for it was playing Christian music. They told him if he stopped playing Christian music, stopped preaching about Jesus Christ, and followed the Communist line, he could continue at the station. But he refused, so they took him and his wife and son to a wall.

They put a gun to the head of his son, and they told the family, "All you have to do is renounce Jesus Christ and we will let you live." Before the father could say anything, his 12-year-old son stood up, with a gun pointing to his head, and said, "I will never renounce Jesus Christ." The Communists killed him in front of his parents.

Then they went to his wife and put the gun to her head. They said, "If you renounce Christ, we will let you live." She replied "Never," and they killed his wife. Because he was an able-bodied man, they put him in stocks and leg irons, and for seven years he worked in a Communist labor camp. Miraculously, he was able to escape across the Cambodian border into Thailand a few months before Ron met him. He had already started a church in the camp to tell the people about the love of Jesus Christ.

The Phony Message

We sometimes wonder why these preachers of prosperity theology in America don't go to the Cambodian border, why they don't go to China and tell those Christians, "Don't you know that God wants you healthy, wealthy, and prosperous? What are you doing in this concentration camp? What are you doing living in a fourth-floor run-down flat? Don't you know that God wants to bless you?"

Obviously those Christians in China, Cambodia, and Laos just don't have enough faith. They just haven't spoken a word of faith or made a positive confession, "named it and claimed it." They must not be as spiritual as we are here in America!

In Africa, in such places as the Sudan, so many Christians are being killed for their faith that they must think the tribulation is in full swing. Somehow the prosperity preachers don't say much there. When they do show up in the area, it's with cameras showing them blessing the refugees with food and medicine—plus a tag line pleading for us to send them more money so they can bless these people with more of their prosperity! Not a single one of these preachers could tell these hurt and dying people to claim health and success and then God would answer their demand. Not one of them has told these people that the key to unlock their faith is to pledge an amount "that God lays on their hearts" to the preacher.

If prosperity theology were truly a doctrine of God, the men and women preaching it should see it as their Christian duty to go to those places and instruct those suffering people in its application. But they never do that because it isn't true. The prosperity gospel is counterfeit. If you cannot preach the gospel to *every* person on earth, it is not the true gospel of Christ. It is a counterfeit religion.

Religious Mind Science

This false gospel is modeled after success formulas promulgated by such people as Napoleon Hill, who has presented his theory in such books as *Think to Grow Rich* and

The Power of Positive Mental Attitude. However, Napoleon Hill tells us that he was into the occult, and that this information was given to him by disembodied spirits and that the system operates under the principle of mind over matter.

Hill and his religious imitators in the pulpit claim that we can visualize our desires, and that what our mind can visualize we can achieve in real life. Our act of visualization becomes a substitute for true faith in God.

The Christian prosperity preacher says that because we are the children of God, He desires the best for us. They ask, "What father would not give his children the best he can provide? How much more will our heavenly Father give us out of what He has to give!" Then they roll out a few dozen "success" stories and the checkbooks come out across the congregation.

The strategy seems to be modeled after some of the multilevel marketing programs that have also captivated many people. These programs offer great wealth, power, prestige, and honors. Every meeting has its buoyant leaders, its testimonials of great success—and also its silent victims.

Yes, a few of the people do make fortunes, but the greatest numbers buy into the program (usually with money they cannot afford), run at full pace trying to duplicate the miracles they heard about at the last meeting, draw in a few friends or acquaintances, and end up broke, discouraged, and with a garage full of soap or vitamins.

Not long ago, Ed attended a Sunday service at the church of one of the prosperity teachers. At the front of the church parking lot were the Lincolns, Cadillacs, and Mercedes of the pastors. It was quite impressive. He took a few moments before he went in to walk around the huge parking lot. First, he noticed that the lot was a mess, filled with potholes in every row. Second, there was perhaps one luxury car in every hundred. And there were at least a dozen clunkers in that same hundred. It's about the same mix as at a multilevel conference.

If you don't have the health and wealth promised, the

promoters' easy out is to shame you with false guilt. They'll say, "You must have sin in your life" or "You don't have enough faith." Thus the victim ends up on a treadmill trying even harder to work the success formula.

This whole philosophy of visualizing and claiming our "inheritance" is religious mind science. It is a counterfeit religion. It is a product of a Western, materialistic mentality, a humanistic philosophy that reduces God to a servant of man, a god that man can manipulate for his own selfish gain. It is the new idolatry.

Paul's View on Riches

Can you imagine what some of these preachers of prosperity theology would be saying if Paul were alive? "Paul, what are you doing in prison? Don't you know that God wants you healthy, wealthy, and prosperous? Obviously you just don't have enough faith, like we do. Paul, you must have sin in your life. You just haven't claimed your inheritance."

What heresy! It was in prison in Rome that Paul wrote much of the New Testament. It was there that God was so glorified that Paul's time in chains is still held in awe 2000 years later. In Philippians he said,

> I want you to know, brothers, that what has happened to me has really served to advance the gospel. As a result, it has become clear throughout the whole palace guard and to everyone else that I am in chains for Christ. Because of my chains, most of the brothers in the Lord have been encouraged to speak the word of God more courageously and fearlessly. It is true that some preach Christ out of envy and rivalry, but others out of goodwill. The latter do so in love, knowing that I am put here for the defense of the gospel. The former preach Christ out of selfish ambition, not sincerely, supposing that they can stir up trouble for me while I am in chains.
>
> But what does it matter? The important thing is that in every way, whether from false motives or true, Christ is preached. And because of this I rejoice. Yes,

and I will continue to rejoice, for I know that through your prayers and the help given by the Spirit of Jesus Christ, what has happened to me will turn out for my deliverance. I eagerly expect and hope that I will in no way be ashamed, but will have sufficient courage so that now as always Christ will be exalted in my body, whether by life or by death (Philippians 1:12-20).

Paul turned his disappointment into God's appointment! He began to share his faith with the whole prison, and Christianity began to spread. Paul understood what Jesus meant when He said that in this life there will be tribulation (John 16:33). He understood that God promised to meet all of our *needs*, but not necessarily our *wants*.

Look at what he wrote from prison a few chapters later. Here he is in a dungeon in Rome, ready to be beheaded, and he says, "Rejoice in the Lord always. Again I will say, Rejoice!" (Philippians 4:4 NKJV). Paul understood where his joy came from: It was not in his material possessions, it was not in his bank account, it was not in his living conditions. Right after he tells us to rejoice, he gives us some more godly instruction:

Do not be anxious about anything, but in everything, by prayer and petition, with thanksgiving, present your requests to God. And the peace of God, which transcends all understanding, will guard your hearts and your minds in Christ Jesus. Finally, brothers, whatever is true, whatever is noble, whatever is right, whatever is pure, whatever is lovely, whatever is admirable—if anything is excellent or praiseworthy— think about such things.

Whatever you have learned or received or heard from me, or seen in me—put it into practice. And the God of peace will be with you. I rejoice greatly in the Lord that at last you have renewed your concern for me. Indeed, you have been concerned, but you had no opportunity to show it. I am not saying this because I am in need, for I have learned to be content whatever the circumstances. I know what it is to be in need, and I know what it is to have plenty. I have learned the

secret of being content in any and every situation,
whether well fed or hungry, whether living in plenty
or in want. I can do everything through him who gives
me strength.

And my God will meet all your needs according to his
glorious riches in Christ Jesus (Philippians 4:6-13,19).

That is the word of God to the church. That is living the
glorious, victorious Christian life. Paul understood that
God *did* promise to supply all our legitimate needs.

Pressing Toward the Real Prize

An evangelist recently told the story of traveling in London. He was scheduled to speak across town in a large
cathedral on Sunday morning. He had only enough money
for bus fare across town to the church, and he wondered
how he was going to get back after the service. But he knew
that God had promised to supply all his needs, so he said,
"God, by faith I am just going to preach, and I'll trust You to
supply my needs to get back home."

He preached his heart out, and after the service people
greeted him and thanked him, and soon he found himself
alone. No one had offered to give him money or to take him
home. So this evangelist began to argue with God. "God,
what are You doing? God, I thought You promised to supply
all my needs!" Then God spoke to him in the quiet of the
cathedral and said, "I did promise to supply all your needs,
and your biggest need right now is exercise. Start walking!"
God knows what we really need.

Paul had learned the secret to life. He had been a highly
esteemed Jew, and he had had all the things which the
prosperity teachers offer. Yet he lost it all. So what did he
say about this? Had he become a failure in his loss? Did he
lack the faith to have good health and great wealth? Listen
to what Paul says.

Whatever was to my profit I now consider loss for
the sake of Christ. What is more, I consider everything
a loss compared to the surpassing greatness of knowing Christ Jesus my Lord, for whose sake I have lost

all things. I consider them rubbish, that I may gain
Christ and be found in him, not having a righteousness of my own that comes from the law, but that
which is through faith in Christ—the righteousness
that comes from God and is by faith. I want to know
Christ and the power of his resurrection and the fellowship of sharing in his sufferings, becoming like
him in his death, and so, somehow, to attain to the
resurrection from the dead.

Brothers, I do not consider myself yet to have taken
hold of it. But one thing I do: Forgetting what is behind
and straining toward what is ahead, I press on toward
the goal to win the prize for which God has called me
heavenward in Christ Jesus (Philippians 3:7-11,13,14).

Paul says that he pressed on toward the goal of the
upward call. What was the goal? What was the purpose of
life he was pressing on toward? "That I may know Christ
and the power of His resurrection." The true goal of the
Christian life is that we may know Christ and be conformed
to His character.

What Is Your Goal?

God may choose to give you financial blessings, and we
believe that God has called some of you to that special
calling. But don't expect God to do that *because* you claim
it as your due; it is merely a gift that God gives to some
people. There is nothing wrong with having financial
wealth, but understand that if God should choose to give
you the ability to make large amounts of money, it is an
awesome responsibility. God will hold you accountable as a
steward of what He entrusted to you.

Our *primary* responsibility as Christians is to rejoice in
the Lord in whatever circumstance we find ourselves, that
we may know Him and the power of His resurrection—just
like Paul.

Where do you get your value as a human individual?
Where do you find your security in life? Is your value based
on your position at work? The title that you have? Is your

security in life based upon how much money you have in your bank? In how many stocks and bonds you own? In how much property you have? Is sickness some of the rain that falls on the just and the unjust, or is it a sign of your spiritual failure? Where does your security really lie?

Consider Job: He lost everything he had in the world and then fell down and worshiped God (Job chapter 1). You may be saying, "That's fine for Paul and Job; they were great men of faith. But you don't know what I'm going through. You don't know the heartache, the disappointment, and the trial that I find myself in today."

You may be wondering whether God has left you. Does God really care about you? You find yourself in a difficult situation medically, financially, or in your family, and you say, "How do I handle that?" You need to simply trust God, who made you and who loves you and who gave His Son for you at Calvary. The One who has done all that for you can deal with all the needs of your life.

Finding What Really Counts

A few weeks before the completion of this manuscript, Ed was raced to the hospital by a team of medics who had responded to a 911 call by his wife, Carol. Ed was in serious pain and struggling for breath when they arrived at his home. He was having what appeared to be another heart attack. Coming on top of a stroke a year-and-a-half earlier, the prognosis was not good. This was now the third time that Ed had made the trip in the back of a Medic One unit.

He spent two days in a critical care unit before the doctors discovered that he had acquired a virus infection in the muscles around his heart, and that the infection had spread to his chest muscles. It has been a long way back, but Ed is all smiles.

> I lay in the back of the Medic One unit, my face covered with an oxygen mask, an IV in my arm, and monitors reading my vital signs across the airwaves to an attending doctor at the emergency room. In the flesh it wasn't a very positive sight. Yet I had such a

positive peace. I knew that I was in the care and keeping of the Master Healer. I knew that I was going to live, either here or in heaven with Jesus. It was hard not to want to go to Him right then. It was just trust in God all the way. I didn't even think about any other option.

Ron tells a similar story of an experience while he was a student in Israel.

Over Christmas vacation we climbed Mount Sinai, where Moses received the Ten Commandments. We had blown out three tires on our Jeep getting there. We were short on gas, so we decided to head toward the Suez Canal to get help from the Israeli military.

It's a long story, but we were caught in the largest raids on Egypt since the Six-Day War, during the War of Attrition in 1969. Later, crossing the desert we blew out more tires on our Jeep. We were stranded for several days without food or water. We drank the water out of our radiator that was rusty mud, eating pieces of wood and chewing on our leather boots to survive.

We were finally rescued by the British Ambassador to Israel (another long story). We ended up flipping the Jeep on our last day as we were heading back. Our three-day trip had turned out to be a two-week odyssey. We went back to Jerusalem, and a week later I began to turn bright yellow. My eyes looked like neon lights. My liver began to swell out of my stomach.

I woke up on Sabbath morning so sick that I could hardly get out of bed. It took me over an hour to get dressed. Finally I got on my motor scooter. (Everyone else had left the school on the Sabbath.) I went through the streets of Jerusalem to Hadassah Hospital and drove up to the emergency room. The doctors knew immediately what I had.

They took blood tests and the doctors said, "Carlson, in another 36 hours you would have been dead." They said this was the worst case they had ever seen of viral infectious hepatitis. They told me I had let it go way too long. They put me in the hospital there in Jerusalem, and I was there for ten days and then had a relapse. It was worse than when I went in.

They transferred me to a French/Arab Catholic hospital in East Jerusalem. I was there for six weeks. At the end of six weeks the doctors said that the only way I was going to survive (because of the damage done to my internal organs) was to put me on a plane and send me home to the United States. Then I would have to stay in bed for the next 10 to 12 months.

The ambulance took me to Tel Aviv. I was put on a plane, and my father met me in New York. He took me home extremely sick.

I had been dating a girl whom I was planning on marrying; in fact I had bought a diamond in Jerusalem for her. When I got home I called her up, but she informed me that while I was away she had fallen in love with someone else and never wanted to see me again.

Then I said, "God, what are You doing? God, why me? God, don't You know how much I love her? God, why do You put me in bed? Don't You know I want to finish my studies? God, why me?"

I became depressed, and for two months I lay flat on my back. I didn't want to talk to anyone. I didn't want to read the Bible. I didn't want to pray. I didn't want anybody to preach at me. I just wanted to be miserable. After two months in sheer frustration, I picked up my Bible one morning and just opened it up. As I looked down, the first verse I saw was Psalm 46:10: "Be still and know that I am God." It was just like God was slapping me across the face and saying, "Carlson, just be quiet! Be still and know that I am God." I replied, "God, what do You want to teach me?"

During those next several months in bed, God began to teach me some things I could never have learned without this time of trial. He began to teach me what it was to have patience. He began to teach me what it was to have full trust and faith, what Proverbs 3:5,6 means when it says, "Trust in the Lord with all your heart and lean not on your own understanding."

When you don't understand why, that's when you have to trust God with all your heart. He began to teach me what it was to have love, what 1 Corinthians 13 means when it says that love bears all things, hopes all things, and endures all things. In fact, God had someone better for me to marry than who I originally thought.

Because of my extreme illness, my father took me to a famous doctor in the Midwest, where we were living at the time. He was 72 years old and had gained great notoriety in the medical profession. He had a large clinic, with a staff of doctors working for him. He had given hundreds of thousands, if not millions, of dollars to Christian work around the world.

I began to share with this doctor the pain and disappointment I was going through. He replied, "Ron, would you mind if I share with you a little about my own life?" I said, "Fine." I learned how eight years earlier his wife had had a stroke and was totally paralyzed. He continued, "Ron, for the last eight years, every day after work I go to the nursing home, go to my wife's bed, hold her hand, and tell her I love her. She cannot speak or move, but I know she hears me, and then I go home to a big house. I wake up in the morning and put a frozen waffle into the toaster, and then I go to work.

"I'm wealthy and I'm a success in my profession. I've given hundreds of thousands of dollars to Christian work. When this happened I said, 'God, why? Why me? Why, when I am ready to retire in the prime of my life do You allow something like this to happen? Don't You know how much I love You? Don't You know how much I have done for You, God?'

"I realized at this point that I had a choice. I could either become *bitter* or *better*. There is only a one-letter difference between the two. You can focus on the 'I' and feel sorry for yourself and become a bitter person, or you can focus on the 'E' which stands for Emmanuel, God with us, and become a better person. Eight years ago I chose to become a better person. I said, 'God, I don't understand why, but I'm going to trust You in whatever You want to do, in whatever You want to teach me, in however You want to use me.'"

That was the turning point for me. I decided that what I was going through was going to make me better, not bitter.

The Loving Blacksmith

Sometimes God is like the blacksmith who takes a rusty, bent-up, twisted piece of metal out of the junkyard. He lays it on the hot coals and begins to heat it up. Then he takes it off the fire, lays it on the anvil, and beats it into a truly useful implement. After that he thrusts it into cold water. When he takes it out of the water it is no longer a rusty, bent-up, twisted piece of metal but a strong, tempered horseshoe, usable for an important purpose.

If you are seeking to grow as a Christian, life is not all health, wealth, and prosperity. Sometimes God wants to conform you to His image. And sometimes that means putting you in the fire, laying you on the anvil and putting you into the cold water. You may not understand why, but when you don't understand, trust in the Lord with all your heart.

> Trust in the LORD with all your heart and lean not on your own understanding; in all your ways acknowledge him, and he will make your paths straight (Proverbs 3:5,6).

> Consider it pure joy, my brothers, whenever you face trials of many kinds, because you know that the testing of your faith develops perseverance. Perseverance must finish its work so that you may be mature and complete, not lacking anything (James 1:2-4).

The J.B. Phillips paraphrase says, "When all kinds of trials and temptations crowd into your lives, my brothers, don't resent them as intruders, but welcome them as friends! Realize that they come to test your faith and to produce in you the quality of endurance. But let the process go on until that endurance is fully developed, and you will find you have become men of mature character, men of integrity with no weak spots."

The real prosperity message is that God wants to give us *Himself.* Paul said in Philippians chapters 3 and 4 that the source of all joy, all security, all value is not based in material possessions. All security and value must rest with God and Jesus Christ.

When you are secure in that relationship it doesn't matter what happens to the things around you. When you center your life in Jesus Christ, no matter what storms of life may be raging around you, you have perfect peace (Isaiah 26:3).

14

Fast Facts on

Roman Catholicism

I t was in 1971, when Ron was traveling through Europe with a group from Youth For Christ, that they were in Berlin and decided to cross over into East Germany. They went through Check Point Charlie and took a train from East Berlin to a town called Wittenberg.

They had a purpose in the trip: They were looking for a very special church there. They walked through the cobble-stone streets and found the church that had been at the center of one the greatest controversies in the history of Christianity. As they stood in front of this church, they saw there a large bronze tablet nailed on the front door.

This tablet was there to commemorate a scrolled paper that had been nailed to that same door in 1517 by a Catholic professor named Martin Luther. On it were listed 95 points of disagreement that Luther had with the dogma of his church.

The scroll of paper which Luther had attached to that door as a Roman Catholic scholar essentially said these words: *"I dissent, I disagree, I protest."* And the Reformation was born. It spread from those very steps across Europe and across the entire breadth of Christendom.

What we must ask is why a biblical scholar in the Roman Catholic church would protest. What was it that he disagreed with in 1517? Were these complaints legitimate? Have they been addressed by the Roman Catholic Church, challenged, or corrected? Have these issues been cleared up, or are they still there today?

The Protestant churches that formed out of the Reformation that began on those steps are still in existence today, and Roman Catholicism is apparently as strong as ever.

It is very evident that some very real differences between Catholicism and biblical Christianity did exist then and do so to this day. It is our purpose to provide a critique of those very real differences so that you may understand exactly what the Roman Catholic Church teaches today and what we find in God's Word, the Bible.

Roman Background

The Roman Catholic Church claims a membership of about 620 million worldwide. In the United States there are about 50 million Roman Catholics, approximately one-fifth of the U.S. population. Catholics represent half the population in Canada.

The Roman Catholic Church has been an important force in world affairs. Nations still send ambassadors to the Vatican just as they do to the great geographic powers.

In the Middle Ages the Vatican was a great political power in Western Europe. Its universities and monasteries became centers of learning. During the sixteenth and seventeenth centuries, Catholic missionaries went to Asia, Africa, and the New World and had a great influence in spreading Western culture.

The Catholic Church certainly influenced art; Michelangelo and Raphael are among the many famous artists brought forth by the Church. The Catholic Church has also greatly influenced music, painting, and sculpture. You see this handiwork among the great cathedrals in Europe today. The Catholic Church operates schools, universities, hospitals, orphanages, and homes for the aged throughout the world.

People see all these positive things and ask, "What is in it that you disagree with so much?"

Let us assure you that it is not with all of the essential, basic issues of theology that we disagree, because Catholics do affirm some of the central doctrines of Christianity. Catholics affirm belief in the trinity, the deity of Jesus

Christ, the Virgin Birth, the sinlessness of Christ, and the atonement on the cross.

Rather, what disturbs us is what Catholics have added to Scripture over the years, so that many Catholics can no longer see the teaching of God's Word in their faith. What they see instead are the ritual and tradition that have been piled on top of God's Word over hundreds of years by the Catholic Church.

Many of these rituals and traditions have kept Catholics from knowing the simplicity of God's true Word. The Catholic Church has added doctrines, traditions, and ideas of men which are not found in Holy Scripture and which are in fact contrary to Scripture.

The Unbiblical Traditions

Some of these Catholic traditions which Bible-believing Christians reject include such teachings as:

The church was built on Peter, who is called first Pope.

The doctrine of purgatory after death to purge a person of sin.

Prayers to Mary and dead saints to mediate on our behalf.

Images to kneel and pray before.

Confession to a priest for absolution of sins.

The Mass and sacraments as necessary for salvation.

Salvation comes only through the Roman Catholic Church.

The Eucharist of the Mass and transubstantiation, the teaching that the bread and wine literally become the blood and body of Christ when taken at Communion.

Penance and the selling of indulgences.

Veneration and worship of Mary, which has greatly increased in recent years.

Holy water.

Canonization of dead saints.

Celibacy of the priesthood.

The Rosary.

All of these are traditions that came into the Roman Catholic Church over the years and became dogmas of the Church. The Church has continued to teach them as if they were scriptural.

It was not until 1545, at the Council of Trent, that the Roman Catholic Church declared for the first time its official position that tradition was now to be equal in authority with God's Word, the Bible.

Once the Church made tradition equal in authority with God's Word, it had the freedom to add more and more traditions, including such ideas as the immaculate conception of Mary, that she was born without original sin, that Mary lived a life of sinlessness, that she was lifted into heaven, that she did not die. In the eyes of Roman Catholics, Mary truly became the Mother of God and the Mother of the Church.

We can add to this lengthy list such concepts as monks, nuns, monasteries, convents, a 40-day Lent, Holy Week, Ash Wednesday, and All Saints Day.

Changing Standards

Many of us will never forget growing up with the one tradition of the Catholic Church that affected Catholic and Protestant alike. Can you remember going to school on Friday and eating in the cafeteria? Remember what you always had? It was fish. Why? Because the Catholic Church taught that it was a sin to eat meat on Friday.

Then along came Vatican II in the 1960's and declared that it was no longer a sin to eat meat on Friday. A significant tradition was changed by a council. One week it was a sin, and the next it was not!

The question is not whether we are antagonistic toward Catholics for their position of faith and their central doctrines. What concerns us are the many additions and adjustments to basic Christian orthodoxy, in the name of papal authority, that do exactly what Jesus warned the religious leaders of his day about.

Jesus on Tradition

In Mark chapter 7 Jesus gave us some very instructive teaching about adding tradition to God's Word. The Pharisees came to Him to complain because some of His disciples were eating their bread with unwashed hands. (The Pharisees and the Jews did not eat unless their hands were washed in the tradition of the elders.)

> The Pharisees and some of the teachers of the law who had come from Jerusalem gathered around Jesus and saw some of his disciples eating food with hands that were "unclean," that is, unwashed. (The Pharisees and all the Jews do not eat unless they give their hands a ceremonial washing, holding to the tradition of the elders. When they come from the marketplace they do not eat unless they wash. And they observe many other traditions, such as the washing of cups, pitchers and kettles.)
>
> So the Pharisees and teachers of the law asked Jesus, "Why don't your disciples live according to the tradition of the elders instead of eating their food with 'unclean' hands?" He replied, "Isaiah was right when he prophesied about you hypocrites; as it is written: 'These people honor me with their lips, but their hearts are far from me. They worship me in vain; their teachings are but rules taught by men.' You have let go of the commands of God and are holding on to the traditions of men." And he said to them: "You have a fine way of setting aside the commands of God in order to observe your own traditions!... Thus you nullify the word of God by your tradition that you have handed down. And you do many things like that" (Mark 7:1-9,13).

This is exactly what has happened with the Roman Catholic Church. Jesus said to the religious leaders of His day that they had made null and void the Word of God by their traditions. Jesus said that man looks at the outward appearance, but God looks on the heart. God knows what the heart is. Do you love God with all your heart?

The religious leaders of Jesus' day couldn't love God with all their hearts, so they created all kinds of outward traditions which they *could* keep so that people could look at them and say they must be religious and spiritual.

The Pharisees created checklists of all the things to do in order to be truly religious. Then Jesus came along and confronted them where it hurt most.

> Woe to you, teachers of the law and Pharisees, you hypocrites! You are like whitewashed tombs, which look beautiful on the outside but on the inside are full of dead men's bones and everything unclean. In the same way, on the outside you appear to people as righteous but on the inside you are full of hypocrisy and wickedness (Matthew 23:27,28).

The Source of Tradition

It is important to understand that as Protestants we are not against tradition as long as that tradition is in accord with God's Word. A Roman Catholic priest came to hear Ron speak at a seminar recently. After the service he introduced himself to Ron and said, "As Catholics, we believe that tradition is equal in authority to Scripture."

Ron replied, "There is nothing wrong with tradition as long as your tradition is concordant with Scripture. But if your tradition contradicts the Bible, you had better start questioning your tradition."

For Protestants, the Bible is sufficient as the standard of our faith. For Roman Catholics, the Bible is *not* the sufficient rule of faith. For them it is the Bible *plus tradition.* While the Catholic Church theoretically adheres to the Scriptures as one source of authority, in actual daily practice it does not encourage its members to follow Scripture but to follow the Catholic traditions.

Unfortunately for the Catholics, it is not even just Scripture and tradition taken together, but the decrees of certain councils or popes. In practical terms, the real rule of faith for a Roman Catholic is not the Bible, or even the Bible and tradition, but rather the Roman Catholic Church itself. It, with its decrees and dogmas, has become the final authority for Roman Catholics.

The Concept of Pope

The Roman Catholic Church claims that the Pope, known as the Bishop of Rome, the Vicar of Christ, the Head of the Church, is God's representative on earth. Pope John Paul II, when he became Pope in 1978, was the 266th Pope of the Catholic Church.

It is important to understand what the Church teaches about its popes. Pope Boniface the Eighth, in his famous Bull ("Unum Sanctum") of 1302, said, "For every human creature, it is altogether necessary to salvation that he be subject to the Roman Pontiff."

In 1870, at the first Vatican Council, Pope Pius the Ninth declared in the doctrine of papal infallibility that the Pope possessed full and complete power and authority over the whole Church, that the Pope can rule independently on any matter which comes under its sphere of the church's jurisdiction, without the concurrence of the other bishops or the rest of the Church, and that there is no higher authority on earth than the Pope.

The Church's authority for elevating the Roman Pope to Supreme Pontiff was derived from one single passage of Scripture. In fact, the authority of the entire Roman Catholic Church must stand or fall on that one passage. It is found in Matthew chapter 16, where Jesus is talking with His disciples.

> When Jesus came to the region of Caesarea Philippi, he asked his disciples, "Who do people say the Son of Man is?" They replied, "Some say John the Baptist; others say Elijah; and still others, Jeremiah or one of the prophets." "But what about you?" he asked. "Who do you say I am?" Simon Peter answered, "You are the Christ, the Son of the living God." Jesus replied, "Blessed are you, Simon son of Jonah, for this

was not revealed to you by man, but by my Father in heaven. And I tell you that you are Peter, and on this rock I will build my church, and the gates of Hades will not overcome it. I will give you the keys of the kingdom of heaven; whatever you bind on earth will be bound in heaven, and whatever you loose on earth will be loosed in heaven." Then he warned his disciples not to tell anyone that he was the Christ (Matthew 16:13-20).

Roman Catholics teach that their authority for claiming Peter as the first Pope, and that they fully derive their authority from him, comes from this single interchange between Jesus and Peter. Throughout history the Roman Catholic Church has claimed that Jesus built His church upon Peter as the rock upon which the church would be built.

But that is not what Jesus was saying. In fact, there is an interesting play on words here. When Jesus said to Peter, "I tell you that you are Peter," he used the term for Peter expressed in the Greek as *Petros* which means a stone or small rock. When He said, "On this rock I will build my church," the word "rock" is expressed in the Greek as *Petra*, which means a massive stone, a foundation stone, a bedrock.

In reality, he was saying, "Peter, you are a small stone, but it is upon this stone, the *Petra*, that I am going to build my church."

What was that foundation rock, the *Petra?* Peter knew what it was. Peter had already affirmed it two verses before when he declared, "You are the Christ, the Son of the living God." And Jesus said in effect, "Peter, you're right; it is Christ that the church will be built upon."

We come across that same use of the word *Petra* in 1 Corinthians 10:4: "[They] drank the same spiritual drink; for they drank from the spiritual rock that accompanied them, and that rock was Christ."

If you examine the Old Testament you will see that the Jews never would have accepted Peter as the Rock. Over 35 times in the Old Testament the term "rock" refers either to

God or to the coming Messiah. Psalm 18:1,2 states this clearly:

> I love you, O Lord, my strength. The Lord is my rock, my fortress and my deliverer; my God is my rock, in whom I take refuge. He is my shield and the horn of my salvation, my stronghold.

Binding and Loosing

When Ron was in Poland, he visited the cathedral in the city from which Pope John Paul II came. It was wintertime, and yet there was a long line of people leading down the street to that cathedral. Ron commented:

> It was a few days before Christmas, and I thought, "That church must be packed out." I made my way past the crowd and went in the back door, and there, inside, the entire church was empty! I wondered what all those people were lined up for, so I went around to the side of the church. There was a little door open, and next to the door was a confessional booth, where the Pope used to take people's confessions. On one side was the priest, listening through an opening where someone else was confessing his sins to the priest. He was telling him to say so many Hail Marys, to say the Rosary, to do certain things for absolution, so his sins would be forgiven.

The authority for claiming this power comes from that same passage in Matthew 16. Right after Jesus said, "You are Peter, and on this rock I will build my church, and the gates of Hades will not overcome it," Jesus said in verse 19, "I will give you the keys of the kingdom of heaven; whatever you bind on earth will be bound in heaven, and whatever you loose on earth will be loosed in heaven."

The Roman Catholic Church claims that this was when and where the papal authority was given to Peter and through him to the bishops and the priests. This was the justification and authority to bind and to loose things on earth, to forgive the sins of man.

But what did Jesus actually mean in verse 19 when He said that He would give Peter the keys to the kingdom of heaven to bind and loose? In chapter 18 Jesus refers to the same thing, but here He is speaking not only to Peter, but to *all* of His disciples, including you and me.

> I tell you the truth, whatever you bind on earth will be bound in heaven, and whatever you loose on earth will be loosed in heaven (Matthew 18:18).

This authority was not simply given to Peter but to *all* of the disciples. What did Jesus mean when He said He gave the authority to bind and to loose?

After His resurrection, He appeared to the disciples and reaffirmed this instruction:

> The disciples were overjoyed when they saw the Lord. Again Jesus said, "Peace be with you! As the Father has sent me, I am sending you." And with that he breathed on them and said, "Receive the Holy Spirit. If you forgive anyone his sins, they are forgiven; if you do not forgive them, they are not forgiven (John 20:20-23).

He gave that authority to *all* the disciples. But how do people have their sins forgiven by His disciples? Peter himself clarified this issue for us:

> He commanded us to preach to the people and to testify that he is the one whom God appointed as judge of the living and the dead. All the prophets testify about him that everyone who believes in him receives forgiveness of sins through his name. While Peter was still speaking these words, the Holy Spirit came on all who heard the message (Acts 10:42-44).

Jesus gave to them and to us, living today as His disciples, authority to *preach the gospel of Jesus Christ* and share the good news with many people. As people respond to the message of salvation by believing in Jesus Christ, we have the authority to say to them, "Your sins are forgiven because you believe in the name of Jesus Christ."

When we preach the gospel and people reject it and turn their backs on Jesus Christ, He gave us the authority as His disciples to say, "You are still in your sins, and you will be lost in your sins unless you repent."

The difference here is the difference between submitting to the authority of a man, the Bishop of Rome, the Pope, or submitting to God, the Holy Spirit, and His Holy Word, the Bible.

The Tradition of Mary

One Catholic tradition which surely contradicts God's Word is the hyper-elevation of Mary. We often see pictures of Mary depicted as the Mother of God and the Queen of Heaven. Catholic people pray their Rosaries to Mary and offer prayers in the Mass to Mary. Today the Catholic church is awash with the worship of and obeisance to Mary.

In May 1991 Pope John Paul went to Fatima in Portugal and placed a crown of diamonds on the statue of the Virgin Mary. One of the news magazines reported that he went there to thank the Virgin Mary for saving his life. Ed remembers the Pope saying at the time that he owed everything he had and everything he was to the Virgin Mary, giving her credit even for sparing his life when he was shot earlier in his reign.

As Protestants we do recognize Mary in a very special way. We honor Mary as the mother of our Lord, Jesus Christ. As Christians we believe what the Bible says: that Mary was blessed to bear Jesus. She was a humble maidservant, a servant of God who submitted herself to God and gave birth to the Savior. We honor her for this. But Roman Catholicism has elevated Mary to a place far beyond that accorded her in Scripture.

What does the Roman Catholic Church teach about Mary that we disagree with? First, the Roman Catholic Church teaches the Immaculate Conception of Mary. This was declared by Pope Pius the Ninth on December 8, 1854. The

Immaculate Conception means that Mary was born without Original Sin, and yet nowhere in Scripture do we find such a teaching.

If she was such an exalted personage, she certainly didn't know it, for Mary herself recognized her need for a Savior.

> Mary said: "My soul glorifies the Lord and my spirit rejoices in God my Savior, for he has been mindful of the humble state of his servant. From now on all generations will call me blessed, for the Mighty One has done great things for me—holy is his name (Luke 1:46-49).

Jesus Himself addressed this issue of His mother having any elevated position of honor.

> While Jesus was still talking to the crowd, his mother and brothers stood outside, wanting to speak to him. Someone told him, "Your mother and brothers are standing outside, wanting to speak to you." He replied to him, "Who is my mother, and who are my brothers?" Pointing to his disciples, he said, "Here are my mother and my brothers. For whoever does the will of my Father in heaven is my brother and sister and mother" (Matthew 12:46-50).

The Catholic Church goes on to teach the perpetual virginity of Mary, that Mary remained a virgin her entire life. Nowhere in Scripture do we find this; in fact it is inconsistent with what we do find.

> Because Joseph her husband was a righteous man and did not want to expose her to public disgrace, he had in mind to divorce her quietly. But after he had considered this, an angel of the Lord appeared to him in a dream and said, "Joseph son of David, do not be afraid to take Mary home as your wife, because what is conceived in her is from the Holy Spirit" (Matthew 1:19,20).

> When Joseph woke up, he did what the angel of the Lord had commanded him and took Mary home as his

wife. But he had no union with her **until** she gave birth to a son. And he gave him the name Jesus (Matthew 1:24,25).

Joseph was told to take Mary as his wife. She lived with him as his wife, in all that this implies. She very obviously could not remain a virgin. She gave birth to other children, the sons and daughters of Joseph.

Coming to his hometown, he began teaching the people in their synagogue, and they were amazed. "Where did this man get this wisdom and these miraculous powers?" they asked. "Isn't this the carpenter's son? Isn't his mother's name Mary, and aren't his brothers James, Joseph, Simon and Judas? Aren't all his sisters with us? Where then did this man get all these things?" (Matthew 13:54-56).

The doctrine of the holiness of Mary goes further. In November 1950, Pope Pius the Twelfth declared what is called "The Assumption of Mary." It is the teaching that Mary was raised, both body and soul, into heaven, where she is exalted as Queen of Heaven.

Near the cross of Jesus stood his mother, his mother's sister, Mary the wife of Clopas, and Mary Magdalene. When Jesus saw his mother there, and the disciple whom he loved standing nearby, he said to his mother, "Dear woman, here is your son," and to the disciple, "Here is your mother." From that time on, this disciple took her into his home (John 19:25-27).

That disciple was John, who was the youngest of all the disciples. John was probably no more than 18 at the time of the crucifixion. In fact, John outlived all the other disciples. He wrote the Gospel of John, the Epistles of John, and the book of Revelation (which he did not write until nearly 70 years after the crucifixion).

If anyone would know about Mary being assumed body and soul into heaven, it would have been John, because Jesus commanded that John take Mary into his own house and take care of her. Yet nowhere in any of his writings did John mention anything about what would have been a tremendous miracle.

The Catholic Church has also elevated Mary as Co-Redeemer and Co-Mediator with Christ. In 1891 Pope Leo the Twelfth declared:

> From that great treasure of all graces the Lord has brought, nothing according to the will of God comes to us except through Mary.

He also said, "No one can approach Christ except through the Mother."

Pope Benedict the Fifteenth called Mary the Mediatrix of God, with all graces. One of the most common Catholic prayers exemplifies this:

> Hail Mary, full of grace, the Lord is with Thee; Blessed are Thou among women, and blessed is the fruit of Thy womb, Jesus. Holy Mary, Mother of God, pray for us sinners now and in the hour of our death. Amen.

When people of biblical times sought to elevate Mary to a place of devotion, even in those Scriptures to which Catholics turn to prove her exaltation, we find the biblical truth of the matter: Jesus repudiated the attempt.

> As Jesus was saying these things, a woman in the crowd called out, "Blessed is the mother who gave you birth and nursed you." He replied, "Blessed rather are those who hear the word of God and obey it" (Luke 11:27,28).

Mary and Jesus

In most Catholic countries, Jesus is portrayed either as a dead man hanging on a crucifix or else as a helpless infant lying in the arms of Mary. He can help no one, so if you want somebody to help you, you need to go through the blessed heart of Mary, and she will understand.

In the cathedral of Quito, the largest Catholic Church in Ecuador, you will see in the center of the altar a crucifix with *Mary* hanging on the cross, shedding her blood for your sins. *Mary,* not Jesus!

This type of thing is happening in many places around the world. Many American Catholics would respond, "I don't believe it; that's not what we do in our churches here." That may be true, but it actually is happening in Catholic countries all over the world, condoned by the Church in Rome. What does Scripture say about this?

> There is one God and one mediator between God and men, the man Christ Jesus (1 Timothy 2:5).

> Jesus answered, "I am the way and the truth and the life. No one comes to the Father except through me" (John 14:6).

Not Mary, not the Pope, not the saints, not the Church, not the sacraments, and not the priests. There is only *one* Mediator between God and man, and that is Jesus Christ.

Those who knew Him best knew the truth. The apostle Peter said:

> Salvation is found in no one else, for there is no other name under heaven given to men by which we must be saved (Acts 4:12).

The Doctrine of Purgatory

Another area of unbiblical tradition is the widely taught Catholic doctrine of purgatory. As taught by the Catholic Church, purgatory is the place of temporary punishment for those who have committed venial sins. When those sins are removed by masses said for them, prayers said for them, and penance done in all forms of work, the person is then released from purgatory and permitted to go to heaven.

What is interesting about purgatory as taught by the Roman Catholic Church is that neither the word nor even the concept of purgatory is found anywhere in Scripture.

In fact, it was not until the Second Council of Lyon, in 1274 A.D., that the Church even gave an opinion about this subject. The Second Council said:

> If those who are truly repentant die in charity before they have done sufficient penance for their sins of omission and commission, their souls are cleansed after death in purgatorial cleansing or punishment. The suffrages of the faithful on earth can be of great help in relieving these punishments, as for instance, the sacrifice of the Mass, prayers, almsgiving, and other religious deeds which in the manner of the Church the faithful are accustomed to offer for others of the faithful.

The doctrine of purgatory was spawned by the theological speculation that some people are not good enough to go to heaven but not bad enough to go to hell, and therefore there should be a place where people can go to be purged and eventually allowed to go to heaven.

No biblical citations are given, no chief theologians are cited, no acts of Jesus or passages of Scripture are referenced. The mere pronouncement of a Papal Council made this teaching the infallible truth and holy doctrine of the Church. It was one of the main heresies that Martin Luther argued against, and was a core issue of the Protestant Reformation.

However, the teaching of purgatory became the best business investment the Catholic Church ever made, for the great influx of money it produced helped build the great Cathedral of Saint Peter in Rome. Purgatory produced the system of indulgences—actions one could perform in order to work off the length of someone else's stay in purgatory. It is a type of time off for good behavior by a person's living relatives, and it continues to this very day.

If you want to help a dead relative in purgatory try to make it to heaven, you need to have Masses said for that person. How do you have Masses said? You pay the Church. For example, if you want a certain number of Masses said and a few years off purgatory, you pay some figure like 500 dollars. If you want bigger Masses and more years taken off purgatory, you give a much larger amount, like 5000 dollars.

Travel around the world to such Catholic countries as Mexico, Central and South America, the Philippines, and southern Europe. Wherever you go, as you walk into humble towns and villages living in abject poverty, what you almost always find in the center of it is a huge Roman Catholic Church crusted with gold and jewels.

How can this be? It is because the Catholic Church teaches that in poverty and suffering we will find salvation. That is why the Christ of Catholicism is still suffering on the cross. That is why Catholics are taught that if they don't suffer enough in this life, they will have to do it in purgatory. That is why the people are poor and the Church is the wealthiest in the world.

No Doctrine of Joy

Ron and Ed were ministering together in the Philippines several years ago and happened to be in central Manila on Good Friday. They stood, with their sons, on a small bridge crossing the street next to the Church of the Black Nazarene. The streets were jammed full of Catholic believers carrying crosses with their impaled Jesus and a glass coffin with a wooden, black Jesus in it. People screamed in agony as they slashed their own backs with whips in which glass was imbedded. It was an unbelievable sight as these people shared the pains of Christ, some even being impaled on crosses themselves.

Yet on Easter Sunday morning, that great day of glory commemorating Christ's glorious resurrection from the dead, the streets were empty and silent. There was no doctrine of joy for these Catholics to celebrate.

Ron was speaking in a large Northwestern city recently, and the lady in charge of the finances for the Catholic diocese came to hear him speak. Afterward she said, "Ron, what you said about purgatory is so true. Here in our state we keep separate ledgers for purgatory. People send in monthly payments to pay for Masses to be said for dead relatives, trying to get their relatives out of purgatory so they might go to heaven."

Why do these people believe such unbiblical things, and what power could make them do such things? They have no choice. Pope Pius the Ninth, who was the first "infallible" Pope, said in 1870:

> I alone, despite my unworthiness, am the successor to the apostles and Vicar to Christ. I alone have the mission to guide and direct the ship of Peter. I am the Way, the Truth and the Life. They who are with me are with the Church. They who are not with me are out of the Church.

More recently, the Vatican Council II in the 1960's declared to the Church:

> This sacred synod teaches that the Church is necessary for salvation. Whoever, therefore, knowing the Catholic Church was made necessary by God through Jesus Christ, would refuse to enter her, or remain in her, could not be saved.

Vatican II went on to say in the 1960's, in the decree on Ecumenism:

> For it is through the Catholic Church alone, which is the all-embracing means of salvation, that the fullness of the means of salvation can be obtained.

If this is what the Catholic Church teaches, and it is, let us be glad that in 1517, on the door of that church in Wittenberg, Germany, an Augustinian Catholic monk had the courage to nail a scroll of paper to the front door which said, "I dissent, I disagree, I protest!"

Faith Alone in Christ Alone

Luther argued for a return to the rock of Jesus Christ and a return to the Holy Scriptures alone for our authority on which eternal truth rests. We agree with Martin Luther when he also affirmed that salvation was through the grace of God. It was by justification by faith alone in Jesus Christ.

What set Martin Luther free was when he was reading Romans and came to this great passage:

> Therefore, since we have been justified through faith, we have peace with God through our Lord Jesus Christ (Romans 5:1).

The just shall live by *faith*, not works. Salvation is *what Christ did for us*. It is not given through the Mass, nor given through the sacraments, nor given through the priests. It is not given by the wafer or by the Eucharist, but only by faith in Jesus Christ.

Celebrating the Mass is the chief act of the Roman Catholic priesthood. Yet there is not one word of such a Mass to be found anywhere in the New Testament. The simple act which Jesus said to do in remembrance of Him has become the continual crucifixion of Christ.

In fact, the Mass, the "unbloody sacrifice," is performed over a hundred thousand times a day around the world! It is designed to offer up over and over again that same sacrifice of Christ, who is said to be present *physically* in the ceremony.

In Catholicism, salvation is claimed through taking the sacrament of the Mass. This claim denies the all-sufficiency of Christ, His atonement and death on the cross as a once-for-all, completed act.

> ... Jesus has become the guarantee of a better covenant. Now there have been many of those priests, since death prevented them from continuing in office; but because Jesus lives forever, he has a permanent priesthood. Therefore he is able to save completely those who come to God through him, because he always lives to intercede for them. Such a high priest meets our need—one who is holy, blameless, pure, set apart from sinners, exalted above the heavens. Unlike the other high priests, he does not need to offer sacrifices day after day, first for his own sins, and then for

the sins of the people. He sacrificed for their sins once for all when he offered himself (Hebrews 7:22-27).

> By that will, we have been made holy through the sacrifice of the body of Jesus Christ once for all. Day after day every priest stands and performs his religious duties; again and again he offers the same sacrifices, which can never take away sins. But when this priest had offered for all time one sacrifice for sins, he sat down at the right hand of God. Since that time he waits for his enemies to be made his footstool, because by one sacrifice he has made perfect forever those who are being made holy.

> Where these have been forgiven, there is no longer any sacrifice for sin (Hebrews 10:10-14,18).

When Christ died once for all time He cried out, "It is finished!" And he stamped "Paid in Full" on our debt.

There is nothing more you can add to your salvation, either here on earth or in some fictional place called purgatory. Christ, the eternal Lamb of God, was the infinite sacrifice who shed His blood once for all time for you. You do not need to go through a priest to come into the presence of God; you can come directly through Jesus Christ.

Tony's Story

When Ron lived in the Philippines, he became good friends with a man named Tony who was raised in Italy. He was ordained by the Pope and sent to the Philippines as President of the Catholic University there.

Tony had his Ph.D. in Catholic Dogma and speaks nine languages fluently. But in 1975 something unusual happened. Tony was saying Mass for a group of nuns in a convent north of Manila. As he drove out the gate of the convent to go back to his rectory in Manila, he noticed a little Protestant Baptist church across the street. He had never been in a Protestant Church in his whole life, having been raised in Italy. Curiosity got the better of him, so he walked into this little Baptist church. The pastor recognized him, and they got to talking.

Then the pastor challenged Tony to simply read the Word of God. Tony said later:

> Here I was, a Catholic scholar, and if you've gone through Catholic catechism, you know that Catholic Dogma says the Bible is the inspired Word of God, so it wouldn't hurt me to read it.

He began to read the Word of God for the next six months. The Word so convicted him that he got down on his knees and asked Jesus Christ to be his personal Lord and Savior. But at that point he had a real problem, because as he continued to study he realized that he would have to go back to Italy and tell the Pope he could no longer remain in the Catholic Church, since it was not consistent with what God had revealed in the Bible.

But his biggest problem was having to go home and tell his Italian mother that he was leaving the priesthood. Yet Tony is now back in the Philippines as a Baptist missionary, in the same place where he was once the President of the Catholic University!

Tony, the Catholic scholar who found Christ, tells people he feels as Paul felt when he wrote Romans 10:1-3. He tells them:

> I pray for their salvation because they have a zeal for God, but not in accordance with knowledge. For they are seeking a righteousness of their own apart from Jesus Christ.
>
> As a Catholic, I had a zeal for God. If you know any Roman Catholics, some of them are the most zealous religious people you'll ever meet. They are working so hard to get God to like them.
>
> I believed in the trinity, I believed in the deity of Jesus Christ, I believed in the Virgin Birth, I believed in the atonement and bodily resurrection. I even taught all those things. But when it came to my salvation, I was trusting my salvation to the Church and to

the Mass, to Mary, and to the saints. I was putting my trust in everything but Jesus Christ.

When I came to realize that there is only one Mediator between God and man, and that Jesus was the way, the truth, and the life, it was a light bulb that finally came on inside me. All of a sudden everything else made sense. The greatest joy in all the world was when I finally stepped out of that bondage of tradition that has been piled on, and discovered the joy and the peace of knowing Jesus Christ personally.

15

Satanism and the Occult Explosion

The Spirit clearly says that in later times some will abandon the faith and follow deceiving spirits and things taught by demons.

—1 Timothy 4:1).

J esus warned us about the last days. He said that in the last days we would see the coming of many false prophets and false Christs, and we are seeing this on an unprecedented scale today.

The Bible also warns us that in the last days before Christ's return we will see many people follow after the doctrine of demons and deceitful spirits, and we are seeing this too as never before.

It is estimated that 50 to 60 million Americans are involved in some form of the occult. A recent survey estimated that over 50 million Americans read their horoscopes every morning to see what they should do that day.

A daily horoscope is found in virtually every newspaper across this country. People are involved in all types of the occult: fortune-telling, the use of tarot cards, palmistry, and numerology. People are openly involved in witchcraft, Satanism, and spiritism. Others are going to New Age channelers, playing with the Ouija board, and attending seances to communicate with the dead.

When troops invaded the home of Manuel Noriega during the liberation of Panama, they found three voodoo witches from Brazil practicing sacrifices to the devil to protect him. When they took him onto the plane in Panama, they found that he was wearing red underwear. In South America, red underwear is a magic, satanic undergarment worn to ward off the evil third eye. Noriega was wearing occult underwear that he believed would keep him from being captured.

The Common People Too

You can't even go to the checkout counter of your local grocery store without confronting the world of the occult. Newspapers and magazines have glaring headlines like "Demons Terrorize Family" or "Horror of the Devil Cults."

People are keenly interested in all kinds of ghosts and poltergeists. They are wrapped up in things like parapsychology, telepathy, clairvoyance, precognition, and ESP. We hear about shamans, spiritism, voodoo, witchcraft, aliens, and UFO's. Hollywood has certainly popularized the world of the occult, with movies like *The Exorcist, The Omen, Heretic, Amityville Horror,* and the *Poltergeist* series.

Over 75 percent of the cartoons on television today are of an occult nature. Look at the cute Smurfs. The whole basis of the Smurfs is that they are a group of little blue characters practicing the occult. They are usually busy creating caldrons of potions of witchcraft, casting spells, and putting hexes on people. We have become so saturated with the world of the occult that many of us have become numb to the reality of what is happening.

In the last days, many people will follow after the doctrine of demons and deceitful spirits. Satan does not come to people today dressed up in a red union suit with horns and a pitchfork and a tail. That's mythology. Second Corinthians 11:14 says, "Satan himself masquerades as an angel of light." He comes seeking whom he may deceive. He comes offering wisdom and knowledge and power, if you only offer up your soul to him.

Many people are drawn in by the power and never realize that Satan has taken their souls. Certainly Satanism has gained great notoriety over the last few years. There were the murders in Matamoris, Mexico, south of Brownsville, Texas, where 16 people had literally been sacrificed to Satan by a drug dealer who hoped that this would gain him protection.

Geraldo Rivera recently did a major special entitled "Satanism in America" which showed the tremendous pull that Satanism has, especially among young people. It is as if Satan has simply taken off the mask and is no longer trying to hide himself. He's simply saying, "Here I am, follow me."

Ron spoke with the executive director of the Satanic Task Force in the United States. She had just come back from meeting with President George Bush in the White House. She said, "You can't believe what is happening in America. Even the White House is deeply concerned with the explosion of satanic activity they are seeing across this country."

In a midwestern city the police and the probation officers met with Ron and said, "What can we do? Every weekend we find dogs and cats being offered to Satan in the graveyards, along with candles and incense, by high school kids wearing satanic symbols."

Even the Young

Young people are getting more involved in satanic activity than ever before. With the increase of dysfunctional families, many young people are into alcohol abuse, drug abuse, and sexual abuse, and are also seeking new kinds of energy and personal control through satanic activity. They believe that Satan will give them power or dominion over their lives and over the lives of those around them.

Many kids go from the dabbling aspect into becoming obsessed with the world of the occult. Soon they begin to take on the characteristics of occult influence, such as wearing occult and satanic jewelry, buying occult books, dressing in black, and wearing white makeup.

They begin to practice the occult rituals they read about or are shown by their friends. They begin to play fantasy role-playing games, such as Dungeons and Dragons. They begin to watch occult movies and videos. They immerse themselves in heavy metal and acid rock music. They openly go into the occult, seeking to take charge somehow in a world they feel alienated from. They step through a veil of darkness, not knowing the evil awaiting them. Some knowingly open themselves up to demonic activity and possession, delving so far into the demonic realm that all hell breaks loose.

What are some of the outward signs of a teenager getting involved in such activity? One evidence is a deep involvement with heavy metal music. We are not talking about rock and roll or Elvis Presley, but satanic lyrics that promote the evil side of life.

What are some of these groups? AC/DC, Iron Maiden, Merciful Fate, Black Sabbath, Slayer, Mötley Crüe, Anthrax, Danzing, Exodus, Grim Reaper, Helloween, Mega Death, Metal Church, Metallica, Celtic Force, Satan, Sodom, and Possessed. All you have to do is look at the album covers to see the incredible satanic influence, let alone listen to the lyrics.

For example, look at Slayer, which is very popular among young people today. Some of the typical lyrics include the following lines from the song "Altar of Sacrifice" on the album "Reign in Blood."

> ... waiting the hour destined to die here on the table of hell, a figure in white unknown by man approaching the altar of death. High priest awaiting, dagger in hand, spilling the pure virgin blood. Satan slaughters ceremonial death, answer his every command.... Learn the sacred words of praise, hail Satan, hail Satan, hail Satan.

These are typical lyrics that young people are listening to in the popular metal groups today. They are not about fun and games, love and romance. They deal with death and terrible evil. Slayer's album "South of Heaven" has a song in it entitled "Mandatory Suicide," which promotes self destruction. There are cases of teenagers committing suicide believing that this is the way to gain power.

Black metal music is not just ordinary music. It is an all-encompassing format that mixes the lyrics with the artist's antics, where groups like Kiss dress up in satanic outfits. MTV videos are showing things that would have caused performers to be arrested a few years ago.

A recent survey by *Billboard Magazine* which is the leading magazine in the music world says that only 9 percent of heavy metal listeners are over 24 years of age. That most kids who listen to it are between 12 and 20. That is the audience that they are targeting.

Satan's Roots

Satan's roots go back into rock music. The contemporary seeds of it come from Mick Jagger and the Rolling Stones. You can go back to some of the early Stones albums in the 1970's and see them posing as witches on the cover of their album entitled "Their Satanic Majesty's Request." Or consider their album "Goat's Head Soup," which shows on the cover a boiling caldron with a floating goat's head in it, which is a satanic symbol. Groups like Led Zeppelin, Black Sabbath, and Ozzie Ozborne from the 70's have promoted Satanism and have become part of our everyday pop culture.

It is incredible what occult jewelry young people are wearing, such as earrings or medallions of the inverted pentagram, the upside-down five-pointed star with the goat's head in the center. It is truly a satanic symbol. The peace symbol, the inverted broken cross, has become a symbol that Satanists are now wearing. For them it represents the upside-down cross of Christ with broken arms, signifying the defeat of Christianity.

Dungeons and Dragons is one of the biggest-selling games in this country for high school and college students. It is a fantasy role-playing game which allows the player to live out, in a fantasy world, all the immoral and perverted desires his mind can conjure up. This is done partly by visualization and partly by calling upon a whole warehouse of occult characters—witches, wizards, demons, and demigods—to aid in living out the immoral behavior within that fantasy world without having to face the responsibility of doing these things in the real world.

Yet sometimes it is hard to separate the reality from the imaginary, and horrible things happen. Dr. Thomas Radke, a practicing psychiatrist and a professor at the University of Denver, has documented 123 cases where Dungeons and Dragons has played a specific role in either murder or suicide among young people.

What Is the Occult?

How do we respond to all this? It is important that we first understand exactly what the occult is. The term "occult" comes from the Latin term *occultus*, which refers to hidden or secret things. It refers specifically to the incursion of a fourth dimension, a spirit realm, into our three-dimensional world.

In prior times the occult referred to knowledge which was available only by going through some sort of secret initiation rites and which could therefore be obtained by only a select few initiates. Therefore in the broad sense of the word even groups like the Freemasons or the Odd Fellows are occult.

But today the word has lost some of that original meaning, since you can walk into any mall bookstore and find an entire shelf on occult books which any kid can purchase. Nevertheless, the idea still remains that occultism is available only to those willing to work for it. Thus we have different types of people being appealed to by occult concepts:

1) Unchurched people, or those who have little interest in organized religion. The occult often appeals to those raised in churches but who had a bad experience in them.

2) Misfits, those who feel alienated from society and seek to know why they feel that way. The occult gives them apparent answers.

3) People whose lives are humdrum and who need some sort of glamorous fantasy. They can say to themselves, "These people may think that I'm a mere checkout teller, but actually I am Frater Honorius, arch-adept of the cosmos!"

4) People who feel lonely or powerless. The occult promises the power to change the universe, and to control the minds and wills of other people. Thus it appeals to those who feel at a loss in their world.

5) People who need to feel elite and exclusive, far above the mundane world. This is why we see so many highly educated, intelligent people get into the occult and the New Age movement. They feel they are on the cutting edge of a new step in human evolution and are far beyond "mere humans."

For the most part these are people who really cannot afford to have their minds any more messed up than they already are. Most of these people are very marginally integrated into society. Thus their involvement with the occult brings them new but different dangers.

Beyond the First Step

Beyond the spiritual dangers of both the cults and the occult, working with occult power invariably introduces the person to the use of psychotropic drugs or consciousness-expanding techniques such as Yoga and TM. This can open the person to psychotic experiences at best, and demon possession at worst!

Advanced occultists believe they can manipulate their own and other people's bodies and minds for "their own good." This frequently leads to highly questionable ethical practices, seduction, rape, physical abuse, and torture and mutilation of animals (and even of people in some of the most extreme cases).

It is sad but true that the pursuit of power (which is what the occult is, in its most blatant sense) leads to megalomania and the desire for yet more power. Sooner or later the occultist must "integrate his dark side" and come to terms with Satan. At this point all bets are off, and criminal or sociopathic behavior frequently result from this alliance. Unquestioning obedience is demanded from such a person; he must be obedient to his own inner demons who tell him to pillage and destroy.

Thus we get the "Son of Sam" types and the Charles Mansons, who are only the tip of a much larger occultic iceberg. They are the ones who slipped and got caught, or who were sacrificed by their merciless spiritual masters. The "smart ones" are still out there, and for them it is still open season.

Mantic Behavior

One major area of the occult is known as mantic behavior. This is the practice of divination, which is seeking to foretell the future through the use of astrology, tarot cards, palmistry, numerology, crystal balls, and tea leaves.

Modern psychics are on television every night with 900 numbers you can call to get your latest fortune or horoscope read.

Black and White Magic

A second area of the occult is magic. We are not talking about sleight-of-hand, illusion, or parlor tricks, but magic in its classical definition. Occultists refer to both white magic and black magic. The difference is that white magic, which is also known as white witchcraft, teaches that there is only one universal source of power, while black magic refers to both a good source and a bad source. Both types of practitioners seek to tap into their source of power to gain power in their own lives and over the lives of other people.

It's very much like the force in Star Wars—the force that Luke Skywalker was always trying to tap into. This kind of universal power source has been picked up by the New

Age movement; Shirley MacLaine and others claim that there is some spiritual force out there. And of course they are right, but they have denied the reality of the true God. When they go after "the force," they are tapping into the world of demons and deceitful spirits.

Any Saturday morning you can see cartoon characters tapping into the force and thereby gaining spiritual power. Young viewers are led to believe that if they can only tap into that force, they will have the same powers.

Some people say that this existed many years ago in movies like *The Wizard of Oz* and *The Wicked Witch of the East.* But the difference is that the Wizard of Oz and the Wicked Witch of the East were presented as evil beings.

Today's young people are being told that the Wicked Witch of the East is basically good, that witchcraft and the force are something good that we can tap into in order to gain power in our lives.

Satanism

A third area of the occult is Satanism itself. It is important to understand what we mean when we talk about demons and deceitful spirits. The Bible says that there is a very real personage of spirit called Satan. It says that he is the serpent of old and that he is out to deceive the whole world.

> The great dragon was hurled down—that ancient serpent called the devil, or Satan, who leads the whole world astray. He was hurled to the earth, and his angels with him (Revelation 12:9).

The devil is real and he has a strategy to bring each of us to destruction. The Bible warns us:

> Put on the full armor of God so that you can take your stand against the devil's schemes. For our struggle is not against flesh and blood, but against the rulers, against the authorities, against the powers of this dark world and against the spiritual forces of evil in the heavenly realms (Ephesians 6:11,12).

Satan was once known as Lucifer, the most beautiful angel, created by God to serve in the very courts of heaven. Yet he sought to exalt himself instead of glorifying God.

> How you have fallen from heaven, O morning star, son of the dawn! You have been cast down to the earth, you who once laid low the nations! You said in your heart, "I will ascend to heaven; I will raise my throne above the stars of God; I will sit enthroned on the mount of assembly, on the utmost heights of the sacred mountain. I will ascend above the tops of the clouds; I will make myself like the Most High." But you are brought down to the grave, to the depths of the pit (Isaiah 14:12-15).

When we talk about demons or evil spirits, we are referring to fallen angels, finite created beings. They were created by God and once served in the very courts of heaven. But because of their rebellion they were cast out of heaven and out of the presence of God.

Adam and Eve, through their rebellion against God in the Garden of Eden, gave Satan access to us. God has temporarily allowed him to have partial influence and control here on this earth, but ultimately God has condemned him and his cohorts to hell for eternity.

God Alone Is Sovereign

Do not ever make the mistake of considering God and Satan as equal or almost equal. *Satan is not equal with God.* God alone is sovereign. God alone is omniscient, omnipotent, omnipresent, holy, and righteous. Satan is a finite created being, a mere fallen angel. He is neither omnipotent nor omniscient. Yet his purpose is to deceive the whole world. Jesus said this about him while rebuking the Pharisees:

> You belong to your father, the devil, and you want to carry out your father's desire. He was a murderer from the beginning, not holding to the truth, for there is no truth in him. When he lies, he speaks his native

language, for he is a liar and the father of lies (John 8:44).

Satan is a liar. When he came to Adam and Eve in the Garden, he said this:

> "You will not surely die," the serpent said to the woman. "For God knows that when you eat of it your eyes will be opened, and you will be like God, knowing good and evil" (Genesis 3:4,5).

That is the same lie that got Lucifer cast out of heaven. But Adam and Eve believed it and were cast out of the Garden of Eden. In the last days people will follow similar doctrines of demons and deceitful spirits.

What does the New Age movement say? You can be God yourself. What do the Mormons say? You can be God yourself. Satan hasn't changed; he simply dresses up his lie in new terms and pawns it off as a new revelation.

Here is what God says about the world of the occult.

> When you enter the land the Lord your God is giving you, do not learn to imitate the detestable ways of the nations there. Let no one be found among you who sacrifices his son or daughter in the fire, who practices divination or sorcery, interprets omens, engages in witchcraft, or casts spells, or who is a medium or spiritist or who consults the dead.
>
> Anyone who does these things is detestable to the Lord, and because of these detestable practices the Lord your God will drive out those nations before you. You must be blameless before the Lord your God. The nations you will dispossess listen to those who practice sorcery or divination. But as for you, the Lord your God has not permitted you to do so (Deuteronomy 18:9-14).

God says very clearly that we, as His people, should have nothing to do with all three categories of the world of the occult.

Astrology

The largest area of the occult today is astrology. It is based upon the supposed 12 houses of the zodiac. Astrological signs are supposedly based upon the time of your birth. The position of the planets, the stars, the sun, and the moon at the time of your birth are used to calculate future events and cycles of good and bad, based upon an astrologist's interpretation of the position of the stars and the planets.

Not only is there no scientific validity to astrology, but it is also one of the oldest pagan practices that God has condemned throughout history. One of the exciting things about God's Word is that it is more relevant than today's newspaper. All these things which we confront in contemporary society God has already dealt with specifically in His Word. Look at these two Scriptures:

> When you look up to the sky and see the sun, the moon and the stars—all the heavenly array—do not be enticed into bowing down to them and worshiping things the Lord your God has apportioned to all the nations under heaven (Deuteronomy 4:19).

> If a man or woman living among you in one of the towns the Lord gives you is found doing evil in the eyes of the Lord your God in violation of his covenant, and contrary to my command has worshiped other gods, bowing down to them or to the sun or the moon or the stars of the sky, and this has been brought to your attention, then you must investigate it thoroughly. If it is true and it has been proved that this detestable thing has been done in Israel, take the man or woman who has done this evil deed to your city gate and stone that person to death (Deuteronomy 17:2-5).

It was such an abomination for Israel to practice astrology—to follow the sun, moon, and stars—that God commanded that people be put to death for doing so.

We do not put people to death today for the practice of astrology because we do not live in a theocracy. But the principle is still the same: God says that these things are an abomination to Him.

Spiritism

Another area of the occult that has gained great popularity is that of spiritism. It is also called channeling, in which a channeler is taken over by a controlled spirit bringing some New Age wisdom. What does God say about this?

> Do not turn to mediums or seek out spiritists, for you will be defiled by them. I am the Lord your God.
>
> I will set my face against the person who turns to mediums and spiritists to prostitute himself by following them, and I will cut him off from his people.
>
> A man or woman who is a medium or spiritist among you must be put to death. You are to stone them; their blood will be on their own heads (Leviticus 19:31; 20:6,27).

Although we don't stone people to death in the church these days, God still considers these things worth His own sentence of death.

Fortune-Telling

God speaks clearly about the area of fortune-telling. Modern-day prophets and prophetesses claim to predict the events to come in your life and in the nation. But God in His Word gives us two tests to determine a true prophet. The first test is found in Deuteronomy 18:20-22.

> A prophet who presumes to speak in my name anything I have not commanded him to say, or a prophet who speaks in the name of other gods, must be put to death. You may say to yourselves, "How can we know when a message has not been spoken by the Lord?" If what a prophet proclaims in the name of the Lord does not take place or come true, that is a message the Lord has not spoken. That prophet has spoken presumptuously. Do not be afraid of him.

So first we must test the prophecy. Does the prophecy come true or not? If it does not come true, you know that the prophet is not of God. The Hebrew prophets of the Old Testament were 100 percent accurate when they spoke from God, or they were stoned to death. It is a very dangerous thing to go around claiming you are a prophet of God. You had better be sure that God is speaking and that you are not speaking from your own mind or imagination.

God warns us of this in Ezekiel 13:3,6-9.

> This is what the Sovereign Lord says: "Woe to the foolish prophets who follow their own spirit and have seen nothing!" . . . Their visions are false and their divinations a lie. They say, "The Lord declares," when the Lord has not sent them; yet they expect their words to be fulfilled. Have you not seen false visions and uttered lying divinations when you say, "The Lord declares," though I have not spoken? Therefore this is what the Sovereign Lord says: "Because of your false words and lying visions, I am against you, declares the Sovereign Lord. My hand will be against the prophets who see false visions and utter lying divinations. They will not belong to the council of my people. . . ."

The second test that God gives us to determine a true prophet is found in Deuteronomy 13:1-5.

> If a prophet, or one who foretells by dreams, appears among you and announces to you a miraculous sign or wonder, and if the sign or wonder of which he has spoken takes place, and he says, "Let us follow other gods" (gods you have not known) "and let us worship them," you must not listen to the words of that prophet or dreamer. The Lord your God is testing you to find out whether you love him with all your heart and with all your soul. It is the Lord your God you must follow, and him you must revere. Keep his commands and obey him; serve him and hold fast to him.

First, you must test the prophecy, and second, you must test the teaching. Are these prophets leading you to the worship of the true and living God, or are they leading you to false gods and a teaching contrary to God's Word? Even if the prophecy comes true, you must test the teaching by the Word of God, as 2 Timothy 3:16,17 instructs.

UFO's

There is a great fascination with UFO's today. What about all these Unidentified Flying Objects? It is estimated that 85 percent of the world's population today believes in the reality of UFO's. In the Soviet Union, 95 percent of the people reportedly believe in the reality of UFO's as some advanced technological civilization coming to save the world.

Surveys show that about 55 percent of Americans believe in the reality of UFO's. The U.S. Air Force has studied UFO's for many years, including the Blue Book study of the 50's and 60's. Much of this information is still classified.

What about UFO's? We don't believe their existence should be denied. There is simply too much evidence today that suggests that *something* is there. It's no longer *whether they exist* but *what they are.*

People give a variety of answers to this quesiton. If you read the books written over the last 10 or 20 years, some people speculate that UFO's are simply a hoax. The problem with this view is that there are too many reliable eyewitness accounts of UFO sightings by people trained to know what is in the sky, including Air Force pilots and astronauts.

Some writers speculate that UFO's are simply natural phenomena. Perhaps people have seen a satellite go over, or a weather balloon, or marsh gas, or a flock of birds, or reflected light from some other object. It is true that many UFO sightings can be explained by natural phenomena, but many others cannot.

Some writers speculate that UFO's are part of some interplanetary civilization. They used to think it was Venus, Mars, or Jupiter, but we have now sent space probes to these planets but have found no life of any kind.

Some writers have speculated that UFO's are intergalactic. Perhaps they come from some solar system within another galaxy that is now seeking to make contact with us. They believe that there are millions of galaxies that evolution must have produced somewhere else. But recent studies appear to show that we are alone in the universe. There is simply no evidence at this point of any extraterrestrial life anywhere in the universe.

Some writers have speculated that UFO's come from some unknown earth civilization. Speculations like the "hollow earth theory" come and go. Perhaps there is a civilization that has escaped the ravages of modern-day society and has developed a high technology. Perhaps it is hidden in some volcano or in the Amazon jungle.

The problem with this view is that today we have several hundred satellites orbiting the earth. We have photographic equipment on those satellites so sophisticated that from 200 miles above the earth it can photograph a mouse running through a cornfield. All of you have been photographed many times over without ever knowing it! Yet from all of this information we have no evidence of any undetected earth civilization.

Some writers have speculated that UFO's are some super-secret weapon. But we have no technology anywhere in the world that can fly at the speeds or angles of UFO's.

Many researchers who study UFO's are now saying that the only possible explanation remaining for Unidentified Flying Objects is that they are of some ultradimensional nature, a spirit realm outside our three-dimensional, naturalistic world.

The Coming of the Antichrist

Our own speculation is based upon the study of Scripture and the study of UFO's, and we emphasize that this is only an educated opinion. What we believe is that we are seeing the world being prepared for the coming of the Anti-Christ on a UFO. In other words, we believe that UFO's are of a demonic realm.

Why do we say this? Because our world today is not

looking for a spiritual messiah; it is looking for a technological savior. If some UFO landed on planet Earth and out
walked a Christlike, benevolent creature, an E.T. who
claimed to be a higher intelligence, who could solve all our
economic and environmental and technological problems,
the world would flock to him.

In virtually all "fourth encounters," where people claimed
to have been taken on UFO's, they all relate the same experience: The creatures told them they could save themselves.
They don't need God because they are gods themselves.
They don't need Jesus as their Savior because they can save
themselves through cyclic rebirth. It's the same old doctrine of demons and deceitful spirits (1 Timothy 4:1).

We need not walk around with a spirit of fear, however.
The Word of God tells us that as we draw near to the Lord,
the devil will flee (James 4:7). It tells us that greater is He
who is in us than he who is in the world (1 John 4:4). In
Ephesians 6:10-18 we are given the armor of God for this
spiritual warfare.

> Finally, be strong in the Lord and in his mighty
> power. Put on the full armor of God so that you can
> take your stand against the devil's schemes. For our
> struggle is not against flesh and blood, but against the
> rulers, against the authorities, against the powers of
> this dark world and against the spiritual forces of evil
> in the heavenly realms. Therefore put on the full
> armor of God, so that when the day of evil comes, you
> may be able to stand your ground, and after you have
> done everything, to stand.
>
> Stand firm then, with the belt of truth buckled
> around your waist, with the breastplate of righteous-
> ness in place, and with your feet fitted with the
> readiness that comes from the gospel of peace. In
> addition to all this, take up the shield of faith, with
> which you can extinguish all the flaming arrows of the
> evil one. Take the helmet of salvation and the sword of
> the Spirit, which is the word of God. And pray in the
> Spirit on all occasions with all kinds of prayers and
> requests. With this in mind, be alert and always keep
> on praying for all the saints.

16

Fast Facts on

Transcendental Meditation

Transcendental Meditation became popular in the 1960's when the Beatles rock group visited India and learned the Hindu practice from its founder, Maharishi Mahesh Yogi. Maharishi discovered that he could prosper by offering a "shortcut to Enlightenment."

Spiritually hungry people in the West were more than willing to buy a simple form of Hinduism and Raja Yoga, called Transcendental Meditation (TM). When Maharishi brought this Hindu teaching and practice to America in the 1960's, his organization was called the "Spiritual Regeneration Movement." His goal was to adapt Hinduism to fit the Western culture. Today Maharishi University in Fairfield, Iowa, is the center of this movement that has spread around the world.

In America alone, over one million people have paid their money and gone through the initiation ceremony to learn and practice Transcendental Meditation. TM has been like a religious chameleon, seeking to blend into the mainstream of Western culture without having its true nature detected. To mask and coverup the true religious Hindu nature of TM, the organization now calls the belief and practice "Maharishi Technology of the Unified Field." The term "Maharishi Technology" is merely a euphemism for the practice of Transcendental Meditation.

The Unified Field

"Unified Field" is merely a pseudoscientific label for the religious philosophy of Hindu monism. To demonstrate the true Hindu nature of TM, you need to look no farther than the writings of Maharishi himself. In his book *Transcendental Meditation*, Maharishi writes:

> To be is of an impersonal nature, so in order to be one's self it is only necessary to come out of the personal nature, come out of the field of doing and thinking, and be established in the field of Being. the impersonal God is that Being which dwells in the heart of everyone. Every individual in his true nature is the impersonal God (pages 267-69).

Maharishi adds:

> The transcendental state of Being lies beyond all seeing, hearing, touching, smelling, and tasting, beyond all thinking and beyond all feeling. This state of unmanifested, absolute pure consciousness of the Being is the ultimate of life. It is easily experienced through the system of Transcendental Meditation (page 46).

The goal of Maharishi is to have you experience the "Unified Field" or the impersonal reality of Hindu monism by practicing "Maharishi Technology," known as Transcendental Meditation. But in order to experience this "Enlightenment," over one million Americans have had to first go through a Hindu initiation ceremony.

The Personal Mantra

After paying an initiation fee, the most crucial and required element in becoming a practitioner of "Maharishi Technology" is the initiation ceremony, in which each initiate is given a personal "mantra" or sacred word upon which to meditate.

Those being initiated into TM are instructed to bring to their initiation ceremony an offering of six flowers, three pieces of fruit, and a white handkerchief. At the ceremony, each initiate takes off his shoes and enters a small, dimly lit room. In the middle of the room is an altar with candles and incense burning. The altar is adorned with a picture of Guru Dev, the departed master of Maharishi Mahesh Yogi. Standing with the initiate before the altar, the instructor recites the Puja, the central feature of the initiation ritual. The Puja is a Sanskrit hymn of worship and is a prelude to imparting the mantra.

The Puja is described for TM instructors in a secret handbook known as *The Holy Tradition*. The English translation of the Sanskrit hymn sung at the initiation ceremony contains the following portions:

> To Lord Narayana, to lotus-born BRAHMA the Creator . . . to Shankaracharya the redeemer, hailed as KRISHNA, I bow down. To the glory of the Lord I bow down again and again, at whose door the whole galaxy of gods pray for perfection day and night.
>
> White as camphor, kindness incarnate, the essence of creation garland with BRAHMAN, ever dwelling in the lotus of my heart, the creative impulse of cosmic life, to that, in the form of Guru Dev, I bow down . . .
>
> Guru in the glory of BRAHMA, Guru in the glory of VISHNU, Guru in the glory of the great LORD SHIVA, Guru in the glory of the personified transcendental fullness of BRAHMAN, to Him, to Shri Guru Dev adorned with glory, I bow down.

Over one million people in the United States have gone through this ceremony, hoping to find ultimate reality and fulfillment! Not only are the initiation ceremony and Puja classical Hinduism, but the mantra or "sacred word" that is received by the initiate in order to meditate is a name of or a name associated with one or more Hindu gods!

In Maharishi's book *Meditations of Maharishi Mahesh Yogi* we read:

> The Vedas [Hindu Scriptures] are a very basic study of the fundamentals of life. That is the reason why, through Vedic hymns, it is possible for those expert in

chanting those hymns to produce certain effects here, there or there. The universe is vast, so many worlds and all that. We do something here according to Vedic rites, particularly, specific chanting to produce an effect in some other world, draw the attention of those higher beings or gods living there. The entire knowledge of the mantra or hymn of the Vedas is devoted to man's connection, to man's communication with the higher beings "in different strata of creation" (pages 17-18).

In the book *The Religion of the Hindus* edited by K.W. Morgan, the following insight into TM is found on page 24:

A mantra is not a mere formula or a magic spell or a prayer; it is an embodiment in sound of a particular deity. It is the deity itself. And so, when a mantra is repeated, the worshiper makes an effort to identify himself with the worshiped, the power of the deity comes to his help. Human power is thus supplemented by the divine power.

Transcendental Meditation, as well as other similar Hindu cults, have had a major influence in bringing Eastern philosophy to the forefront in America.

The Headship and the Consequences

It is important to understand the dire consequences of adopting this Hindu and Buddhist philosophy as a basic worldview for life and daily practice. Calling upon other gods, chanting their names, and emptying oneself of self will surely bring a person under the headship of whatever god he or she embraces. *To embrace a pagan deity is a sure guarantee that you will soon be the surrendered servant of that deity.*

For a Christian, there is only the true and living God. All the rest are false gods who can only lead their followers into the pit of hell. To state it in even simpler terms, *what is not of the true God is of the devil.* People who think they are uniting with the cosmos by ridding themselves of self are actually being given over to demonic forces.

Christians who think they can dabble with TM and still walk within the Christian faith are fooling themselves. The Word of God is clear on this:

> Do I mean then that a sacrifice offered to an idol is anything, or that an idol is anything? No, but the sacrifices of pagans are offered to demons, not to God, and I do not want you to be participants with demons. You cannot drink the cup of the Lord and the cup of demons too; you cannot have a part in both the Lord's table and the table of demons. Are we trying to arouse the Lord's jealousy? Are we stronger than he? (1 Corinthians 10:19-22).

> The Spirit clearly says that in later times some will abandon the faith and follow deceiving spirits and things taught by demons (1 Timothy 4:1).

Those who claim there is no God or that we are all one god in unity, but who worship these demons, have missed one very critical point: These demons are deceiving spirits who really know the truth but are masking it for their own purposes. They are the fallen angels cast out with Satan from the presence of the true and living God.

> You believe that there is one God. Good! Even the demons believe that—and shudder (James 2:19).

The Christian's only proper response to such deceiving attempts by Satan is the same response that Christ gave to the tempter:

> Away with you, Satan! For it is written, "You shall worship the Lord your God, and Him only you shall serve" (Matthew 4:10 NKJV).

For further information on seminars, videos, and casette tapes by Dr. Ron Carlson, please contact:

Dr. Ron Carlson
can be reached at:

Christian Ministries International
7601 Superior Terrace
Eden Prairie, MN 55344

Ed Decker
can be reached at:

Saints Alive Ministries
P.O. Box 1076
Issaquah, WA 98027
Phone: (206) 228-0175
Fax: (206) 228—0235